ORGANIZING TO Win

ORGANIZING TO *Win*

The Art & Science of Running for Office

JIMMY TICKEY

PYP **Publish** Your Purpose

Publish Your Purpose
141 Weston Street, #155
Hartford, CT 06141

PYP **Publish** Your Purpose

The opinions expressed are solely those of the Author, and not necessarily those held by Publish Your Purpose.

Quantity sales and special discounts are available on quantity orders by committees, associations, and for educational purposes. For details, and press inquires, contact info@organizingtowin.com.

Edited by: Kelsey Spence
Cover design by: Nelly Murariu
Author Headshot by: Jennifer Lynn Photography
Typeset by: Medlar Publishing Solutions Pvt Ltd

ISBN: 979-8-88797-196-4 (hardcover)
ISBN: 979-8-88797-200-8 (paperback)
ISBN: 979-8-88797-201-5 (ebook)

Library of Congress Control Number: 2025913718

First edition, January 2026.

Publish Your Purpose is a hybrid publisher of non-fiction books. Our mission is to elevate the voices often excluded from traditional publishing. We intentionally seek out authors and storytellers with diverse backgrounds, life experiences, and unique perspectives to publish books that will make an impact in the world.

"One of the penalties of refusing to participate in politics is that you end up being governed by your inferiors."

Plato

CONTENTS

★ ★ ★

PART III: MANAGING THE CHAOS

PART IV: NOW WHAT?

INTRODUCTION

★ ★ ★

The American story has been written by the people who show up, speak out, and organize, especially in challenging times. If democracy is worth fighting for, then it starts with each of us. Our democracy hangs in the balance, with a billionaire class calling the shots in a broken campaign finance system, all while pushing for unreasonable tax cuts to benefit the richest corporations. Meanwhile, generational programs working families count on are questioned and slashed. Prices for essential items rise, as everyday people work harder and harder to make ends meet. The economic deck is stacked against working people as they are nickel-and-dimed, and this in part leads to growing cynicism about those writing the rules in our government.

Our democracy was created with the express call for an engaged citizenry, one where citizens participate, hold officials accountable, and even run for office. My hope is that during our time together you will feel included, informed, and inspired to get off the sidelines, support causes you care about, and enter the political arena.

I'm writing this for people who want to understand the political process so they may stand up for their values by organizing a campaign. It's for those who feel they are on the outside looking in and want to play a more active role. This will be helpful if someone feels different from their current representation and they want to run for office, particularly in local or state elections.

I never thought for a moment I'd be involved in politics. Growing up in a middle-class family in Connecticut's blue-collar, working-class community of the Naugatuck Valley, I saw government figures on newspapers sitting atop our kitchen table. My mom, who worked in public education, and my dad, who was in and out of manufacturing, grew up similarly: civically engaged, but not politically involved. Kitchen table conversations with my parents—and my big sister Nicole—were never partisan, but the issues of the day were discussed: how school was going, where we might go for summer vacation, and when big box-stores were starting to come to our quiet town. As a kid, so much is heard without truly understanding the meaning of the rising price of goods, family dealing with struggles, or why some politician was caught in a scandal.

No matter what was happening, my parents voted in every election, and always cast their ballot for the *best person*; they were true unaffiliated voters—not tied to any one political party. Every Election Day, I would join my parents at our polling place—conveniently my elementary school—and we would walk in as candidates glad-handed voters. At the time, I had no idea who these people were, as I was flinging around a superhero action figure and thought it was cool to be in my own elementary school at night. This was *my* elementary school we were voting in. I would go into the voting booth with my mom (superhero action figure in hand) and pull each lever for candidates she selected, grab the metal arm and slide it across, locking in her vote and feeling the *swoosh* of the curtain opening. It was as if I could shout, "Hello, out there; I just carried out my mom's American duty to vote!"

Of course, as a child I didn't know about issues or candidates, but I liked the feeling of voting. Our voting mechanisms have changed since then; we now fill in bubbles like it's a standardized test. Voting feels less exuberant, but perhaps that's fitting since, as an adult, I realize the choices we face on the ballot are serious, and no superhero is coming to save us.

People tell me that entering politics is intimidating. "That must be for *others*, not me," many think, because they see how negative political campaigns can be, or the enormous amount of money in politics is a turn off. Others watch campaigns from a distance and think they don't belong, otherwise known as imposter syndrome. Somehow, they think they don't have what it takes. Have you ever felt that way?

★★★

We need fresh voices like yours to engage in the process so we have a government of the citizens.

Most of all, people don't know what they don't know, and with the decline of teaching civics, people may not be aware that public service is an option. Collectively, this stops people from pursuing a path of getting involved and running for office.

We need fresh voices like yours to engage in the process so we have a government of the citizens. During periods of political instability, and with increasing polarization, an informed and engaged citizenry is even more important. Without meaningful civic participation, we risk the very strength of our democracy, as some wonder if we will keep it at all. With so much at stake, we need *you* to engage and run for office. Our time together is going to help you so when you run, your efforts will become *something special*; one that benefits our democracy.

I bring twenty years of experience organizing campaigns at a very young age at the nonprofit, local, state, and federal levels. I've seen campaigning from every angle: as a volunteer, campaign manager, political party leader, senior staff to officials, and an office holder myself in a *very* challenging district, given the partisan divide. My personal journey is another story—this is about *you*. So let's sit down side by side and talk about your participation in our democracy.

I will take you behind the scenes, and give you advice I've offered to activists, staff, and candidates as we move through your journey. Along the way, I will share experiences and lessons as they are relevant. This is a how-to book, and I am talking with you—yes, *you*!

This is a companion guide for how you can meet the moment as you participate, organize, and lead. It's the book you need while door knocking, fundraising, crafting a message, managing campaigns, dealing with obstacles, running for office, and leading political organizations. We will discuss how to get involved in meaningful ways, the decision to run, break down complex campaign topics, outline action plans, and deal with leadership strategies:

- Part I reviews the first steps to running for office: learning your district, knowing what drives you, understanding what it takes to win, and establishing your team.
- Part II deals with the most critical pieces of a campaign: contacting voters, mobilizing volunteers, fundraising, and messaging.
- Part III prepares you for the chaos: weathering storms, managing people, scheduling, and getting your voters to the polls.
- Part IV guides you in your future: your first one hundred days in office, building coalitions, and the importance of year-round organizing.

This book is a conversation between us, the kind everyone has with someone experienced when they want to get more involved. Should you not feel ready to run for office yet, but want to help others, there will be many lessons for you too. If you are already in the political arena, we will sharpen your skills and enhance your approach to organizing. We will cover the who, what, where, when, and why of campaigning so you understand the framework and the strategy behind it.

Let's start with a secret, just between you and me: The reality is the best *candidate* does not always win. Truly great candidates *can* prevail over a lousy campaign. Similarly, a well-organized campaign *can* overcome its own weak candidate. Often, the political environment in which you are enveloped is decisive, and so it's the greatest candidate *or* campaign—whichever is greater—in the right environment that wins.

"But what does a great candidate or weak candidate even mean?" you might ask. A candidate is at the center of their campaign, putting themselves forward to voters with a vision for the future. I've seen a lot of campaigns, and it takes a lot to impress me these days. I also have developed a keen sense of what makes a great candidate. Together, we will review timeless strategies, new tactics, and many creative ideas for your campaign with actionable guidance.

Organizing a campaign is part art and part science, and you can make it your own. I encourage you to return to relevant chapters as you organize your campaign, and I hope you will pass this book onto someone else on the outside looking in as if to say, *we need you to meet this moment.*

PART I

AT THE TABLE

TWO EARS AND
One Mouth

★ ★ ★

When I graduated from college during the 2009 Great Recession at the age of twenty-two, I had friends who knew I would be coming back home to Shelton, Connecticut, and thought I could volunteer for a local mayor's race. *I did not know one thing about politics.* In fact, I never even studied political science. But, with love for my hometown and time on my hands, I thought this would be a good experience to learn about politics and government. I pictured a campaign with rooms full of volunteers, the kind of well-oiled machine you see on TV, complete with slick offices and loads of staff.

So you can imagine my surprise when, on my first day on an unseasonably warm spring morning, I realized the extent of this campaign was me, a clipboard, and the candidate in his pickup truck. Located on a winding backroad of town, we were to go door knocking. *Door knocking?* I thought. *We are going to go house to house as if we were solicitors?* I still remember I didn't even bring a bottle of water with me, a rookie mistake.

I learned campaigns are hard work, harder than people think, and messier than any TV show has portrayed. I also learned that one person can make a difference, especially that first person who begins the effort. Campaigns at the federal or state-wide levels will eventually have those rooms of volunteers, but so many local races do not receive the attention they deserve despite local decisions impacting people the most.

A term you will hear on campaigns is turnout. Turnout is the amount of people who vote on Election Day. Undoubtedly, turnout is the highest at the presidential level, often exceeding 75 percent of eligible voters exercising their right to vote. For state elections, where individuals cast a ballot for governor, turnout will usually exceed 55 percent. The local level—your town and city—will have the lowest turnout, usually around 30 percent. That means for every ten eligible voters, you are *lucky* if three vote.

Presidential

 75%

State

 55%

Local

 30%

It used to be that "all politics is local," but lately it's become national politics all the time. Some voters will only vote for those big federal elections, and drop off (meaning they will not vote) in local elections. We've all seen community campaigns encouraging people to eat local and shop local because there is a recognition of how important it is for people to engage in their community and support local businesses. How about we add *vote local*? Local elections have the lowest turnout rates, though they have the greatest impact on our lives. Just think of your roads, bridges, school system, first responders, libraries, economic development, open space and zoning ordinances—all of these are under the purview of your locality. More work is needed to inform people that simply showing up locally can make a difference.

In thinking about running for local office, it helps to be rooted in your community. Being born and raised in the town comes with

In order to best position yourself, make it a goal to show up and accomplish something *before* you run for office.

advantages like a known network, but if you are not from the town, then get involved *first*; don't just parachute into town and run. In order to best position yourself, make it a goal to show up and accomplish something *before* you run for office.

My hometown of Shelton, Connecticut, is a city with about 43,000 residents; a mill town on the Housatonic River that used to be the center of the manufacturing industry in a region called the All-American Naugatuck Valley. Over decades, those factories shuttered, and they sat idle as the town developed its main commerce corridors. While I was in college in New York, the City of Shelton was rocked by a federal probe during a public corruption scandal. The findings of that investigation created a feeling in town that to get ahead you needed to be a favored and well-connected good ol' boy.

Politically, Shelton was as deep-red Republican as they come. Local Democrats were unable to unseat those in power, and after I managed that mayoral race, I decided I would run for office myself in the next local election at the age of twenty-four. I felt a calling to put my own voice forward, a perspective I did not think was reflected in my local government. I ran and earned a seat at the table of our budgeting board, which was a way to learn how the town functions, where money flows, and how departments operate. Two years later, I ran for the Planning & Zoning Commission, and won. I went on to be re-elected many times, and in my latest election, earned more votes than any local Democrat on town record. Having never studied any of this, and often being the youngest person in the room, I learned by showing up, respectfully asking questions, listening to answers, keeping in touch with the public, and never being outworked. Throughout our time together, I will share with you many of the lessons I learned.

UNDERSTANDING YOUR DISTRICT

As I was running for office myself, I began to understand there was a group of individuals from my local political party, the Democratic Town Committee, who supported local candidates. It was a group of hard-working folks who had not won a major seat in decades, and optimism was in short supply as they pressed on with each election.

I met local party members and leaders who I am still close with to this day, including one of the first people I met at the start of my political journey: Bob Lally. Bob was a no-nonsense gentleman in his seventies who owned a popular independent hardware store in town. He was a Democrat, but not so partisan that he wouldn't work across the aisle. Bob had respect from all corners because he was viewed as a fair broker who truly cared about people. He was the most senior member of the local Democratic group, and he was generous with his time for those serious about getting involved. When I began to express interest in learning how the local party functions, he gave me advice at the breakfast table one morning: "Remember, you have two ears and one mouth." *That meant hush up and listen.*

By attending public meetings like the Board of Aldermen (our legislative body) and political party meetings, I learned about local government, both the operations as well as the personalities. Piecing together how these organizational structures and people worked with one another, I asked questions, and listened when people spoke. I then would ask, "Who else should I be meeting with?" You may be surprised that people are happy to connect you with others as you are information gathering.

In getting involved, you may find there is tension between those viewed as the political veterans and the newcomers. I began to talk with our longtime Democratic Town Committee chair, Dave Gioiello, about organizing efforts and an increased digital presence for the group. While we had different styles, we both wanted to revitalize our local party. In that common goal, we ended up working well together, blending his know-how of the political process and my ideas for the future.

Approach your early involvement with an interest in learning about your community while being inquisitive about processes and people. Look at the data available to you, like census figures, to understand indicators of your area, from major employers to demographic breakdowns, median incomes, and projected growth data points. Ask questions, learn from those who are willing to share their experiences, and keep your head down doing the research to understand the lay of the land. I realize not everyone will be so welcoming, and you'll need to work that much harder to get involved. Sometimes, you may need to work around unmoving people to get to those who are willing to help. Surveying the environment will take time, but it is a meaningful way to learn, and it's worth the effort.

For those who feel on the outside, realize there is no better lens than an outsider looking in—watching the movements, hearing the conversations, and learning how this works. With a sense of your district, you'll begin to understand the organizations, civic groups, and people that make a difference every day for families in your area. Let's review how to engage locally, advocate within government, and explore the two ways to hold a role in politics.

★★★

For those who feel on the outside, realize there is no better lens than an outsider looking in—watching the movements, hearing the conversations, and learning how this works.

WAYS TO ENGAGE LOCALLY

There's no one like you, and *you* have something special to bring to your community. For those wanting to get more involved, look no further than your locality. Here are some ways to make a positive local impact:

- Volunteer on a nonprofit board.
- Spend time on a local committee, like a street clean-up.
- Mentor in schools, or teach youth organizations.
- Help at the senior center.

- Make or gather food for those at your local shelter.
- Join community, block, co-op, or fraternal organizations.
- Participate in your chamber of commerce and networking groups.
- Engage in your church community or affinity groups to which you are aligned.
- Find a refugee or immigration group and offer assistance.
- Donate to book sales, food drives, and philanthropic efforts.
- Learn about an issue, and meet others who are organizing around it.
- Meet a local candidate and help them with their race.

UNDERSTANDING THE WORKINGS OF GOVERNMENT

As you are getting involved, use your voice through advocacy to test the very system you want to be a part of. For those who are witnessing the issues they care about under attack, you must channel that anxious energy into action. *Organize, do not agonize!*

To advocate legislatively, you can circulate petitions, write letters, and make phone calls to reach officials. A series of calls on a policy matter can lead to a working group, and never underestimate the power of a team working together. I've seen groups turn public opinion, real or perceived, on local zoning decisions and state administration policy. If you are in city hall or at the state capitol, then you may be able to grab a legislator's ear for a moment. Once you have their attention, connect the issue to their district, and use facts while making your point. You can also advocate by testifying at a public hearing. For this you'll need to contact the committee or office of jurisdiction and get on the docket to address the voting body at a set date and time. For advocacy campaigns, perhaps for a local referendum question, you'll learn ways to reach voters like in an electoral campaign, which we will review. You'll learn a lot about government by playing in this advocacy space, and understand what authority officials have, and don't have. You'll also learn there are two ways to serve in a public position: get appointed, or get elected.

ONE WAY: APPOINTED ROLES

Appointed roles are chosen by key elected officials. For example, a mayor may have several appointments to make, from the walking trails committee to their own executive staff. Other times, a local legislative body like a council may appoint people for roles, like a conservation commission or board of zoning appeals. Similar to local government, one can also be appointed to a state board or commission by state appointing authorities. If you want to pursue an appointed role, learn the steps to reach that proper authority. Some may have requirements based on party-identification to ensure there are Democrats, Republicans, and unaffiliated people on the commission. Meet current members and those who previously served in that role to learn how it functions. You'll find joining an appointed board, which can be anything from a local sewer commission to a statewide tourism commission, is a way to get involved. One benefit of an appointed position is being in public service without needing to run for office, so you can learn, build name recognition, and gain knowledge for the future.

ANOTHER WAY: ELECTED ROLES

Elected roles are those positions in government in which voters decide. You will need to know if you are in a partisan election or not; most elections will be partisan in nature, meaning the ballot shows your party affiliation. Some towns and districts elect a mayor, council, and board of education, while others conduct elections for even more, including library board, planning & zoning commission, and taxing board. Of course, there are elections for legislative seats including state representative and state senator who represent people across several towns at the state level.

Local government meetings are open to the public, so attend them, read meeting minutes, and advocate for what you believe in. If you disagree with the way the town has been handling funding for the school system, and you see the board of education is up for election this year, then that may be a path for you. If you feel the priorities of your neighborhood are not being addressed on the city council, then your voice may be needed there. Through curiosity and involvement, you'll formulate a vision of where this could take you.

When something needs attention, many will say how *someone* should fix this; but you'll find yourself saying *I should fix this*. If you have that desire to roll up your sleeves and meet the moment, then run for office. With a passion for your district and a purpose that drives you forward, you can show up and form a campaign in your own way.

Let's get started . . .

WHAT'S
your Why?

★ ★ ★

W hat drives you in this endeavor of getting involved? It's a hard question to answer because it requires some thinking, and it's possible you don't know yet. But if you search hard enough, you'll identify the piece of you that makes you, *you*. Answering this question does not need to be your life's purpose, but it needs to be derived from an authentic place within you for this moment we are in. That driving force could be a passion for reducing inequality in real ways for your community, making your government more responsive, or bringing more joy through arts. In other words, ask yourself what your passions and interests are. Then, connect that to what people want, and need. Now you are onto something.

I had been involved in local nonprofit organizations before I ever thought of running for office, which helped me understand the needs of residents in my community. The Naugatuck Valley is a working-class region south of Waterbury, Connecticut. It's a tight-knit community of towns where people still know each other and there is a great value placed on family and tradition. The nonprofits in my community formed a close network of support for working families who live paycheck to paycheck. From charity car washes and garden clean-ups, youth leadership programs and allocating grants for local groups, I met leaders around boardroom tables—political, business, and civic—and learned how a life of service is a path one could take.

At a young age, I chaired the Valley United Way Board of Directors and community campaign and worked with our board and volunteers to raise several million dollars for our programs, helping asset limited, income-constrained working individuals. For our community, it was a lot of money. I never thought I'd run for public

⭐⭐⭐

You'll know you're on the right path of finding *your Why* when you are working toward something, improving your community, or making life better.

office, so I was happy to just be involved at a young age; meeting community leaders, volunteering on weekends, and helping neighbors. Years later when I started knocking on doors while running for office, people remembered me from those earlier experiences.

You'll know you're on the right path of finding *your Why* when you are working toward something, improving your community, or making life better. In fact, others will start coming to *you* as the go-to expert in a certain area you've focused on. As you begin your journey of public service, you'll be achieving something *before* you decide to run for office. I know that may feel daunting, but you might be surprised if you take an inventory of what you've created, accomplished, or achieved so far in your community. By making your mark before running for office, you are showing you care about your community, can get things done, and have a record of results.

Your involvement before running for office will start to tell a story of who you are. Often referred to as name recognition, there's a benefit to people knowing you, or at least something about you, before you run. Are families already talking about your good work? This kind of exposure begins to get people chatting about you and how you are regarded—a hard worker, a reformer, an activist. People want their elected officials to do something, and you can show them you are *already* in the community, doing good!

Too often, people want to stop something, harm a group, or blame others, and those negative views won't propel you forward. A positive plan, like adding workforce housing, funding schools so students can compete in this economy, or creating a project-labor agreement for a mixed-use development are proposals you may believe in. You could have a vision for a downtown and run for local office to realize a transit-oriented development that enhances small businesses and has residences for young people. You might want to advocate for a neighborhood in the district that is often overlooked, bring about environmental policy, find governmental efficiencies, or build something new to serve constituents. All of these efforts improve the quality of life for people; they can make life easier, healthier, more affordable, more convenient, generally happier, and even better.

AUTHENTICITY

Merriam-Webster defines authenticity as "not false or imitation; true to one's own personality, spirit, or character." You've met people who exude this, and others who don't. Be the candidate from whom people walk away not only understanding your goals but feeling like they want to *join you* in your pursuit.

Authenticity is derived from feeling a passion for your purpose; that you are enthusiastic about your purpose! Thinking through the work you've already been engaged in will help illuminate what drives you. You don't need to come out on your first day of campaigning with every policy position, but you need to have a sense of who you are, what you would do in office, and why you're the right person for the role.

One time, I was door knocking with a local candidate, and they were asked about an issue in such a way that the voter didn't make their own position known, to which the candidate replied, "I don't know," with a quick shrug and said, "Whatever you think. What do you think?" This was a quick reaction to dispose of the question and starkly try to answer however the voter wanted. The voter was turned off, and the candidate was annoyed to be asked a question without a clear suggestion of an answer.

Those are the moments when authenticity (and a little preparedness) shines through. Even if the candidate did not have strong feelings on the issue, they could more authentically bring the voter through a thought process and ask for their opinion. For example, "I have not heard much about that issue, so I haven't considered it. What do you think about it?" Or, "Tell me more about that. What do you mean?" The campaign will be tough, and serving in office will be even more challenging, so approaching this from an honest place will drive you forward each day.

ASK YOURSELF, WHY?

People run for office for different reasons. Perhaps a candidate was running unopposed and someone else believed in giving voters a choice, so they put their name forward. They may not actively campaign, but they will volunteer their name to offer voters a choice on the ballot. Others run to advance a specific policy position, not expecting to win but wanting to further an issue.

Sometimes, people are asked to run. If you are being asked to run, think about why that is, and consider the request thoughtfully. Reflect on what the needs of the district are and what you could bring to the table. Do the needs of the district match your experience and values? Local leaders may see something in you that you don't yet see in yourself, and you should consider that. While there are many reasons why people run, for our purposes, we are running an authentic candidate like you, and organizing to win.

Voters are smart, and if you aren't passionate about making a difference, your candidacy may not withstand the scrutiny of the campaign. Do you have an idea of something you want to fix or accomplish? Think about a vision you have for your town, district, or state, and picture how things *could* be. How do *you* want to meet this moment? You should ask yourself these questions when you are thinking of running for office:

- Why do I want to serve in public office?
- What do I specifically want to achieve in office?
- Can I make time every day to campaign?
- Is my family supportive?
- Am I willing to raise funds?
- Do I understand I will be under scrutiny?
- Does my professional role allow me to run for office?
- Do I have any deficiencies or negatives in my personal or professional life?
- Is my social media footprint something I am proud of?
- Do I live in—and understand—the district for which I am running?
- Do I like meeting and talking with people?
- Do I know who my opponent(s) will be, and am I prepared to face them?

When thinking about *why* you want to run, the following are all good reasons:

- You have a set of ideas you want to put into practice.
- You want to make life easier, healthier, more convenient, more affordable.
- You see a problem and want to fix it.
- You aim to alleviate a burden people in the district are facing.
- You have a policy or program you'd like to enact.
- You represent the values of your district, and you can point to exactly what those are.

All of these have a commonality: authenticity and a commitment to improving quality of life; being positive and centering yourself around a purpose.

If your reason was that you are romanticizing a big office you could run for later, or perks you think you'll get, then your candidacy is not going to give voters the sense you are an authentic candidate. It may not be known at first, but it will be known in time. If you find yourself thinking you want to remove people's freedoms, have a personal vendetta against others, wish to simply collect a title, or are bored and looking for something to do, then get a hobby because we need more candidates with a positive purpose.

LOCAL—AND COUNTY—OFFICE

Local leaders do their best to meet the needs of residents, often with limited resources given budget contraints. These races are closest to the people, and many towns and cities have a chief elected official, often called a mayor or first selectman. Research your own town, as some forgo a mayor and have a nonpartisan town manager, serving with a local legislative body that oversees the town's operations. Town legislative bodies, called alders, councilors, or even representatives, are people who make up the highest local legislative board overseeing the town, passing budgets, and approving ordinances. There are other positions too, like treasurer, city clerk, board of education, planning & zoning, and board of finance, among others.

Many states have county governments, and they will have executive county leadership, often called county commissioners. County governments carry out state and federal laws and provide services across many towns in a geographic area.

STATE OFFICE

States have their own constitution, and they have the authority to elect a governor, lieutenant governor, and often other offices, including attorney general, treasurer, secretary of state, judges, and, of course, a state legislature who set policy and budgets at the state-level. Some legislators—both state senators and state representatives—may be full-time positions, while other states opt for a part-time legislature that is only in session for several months of the year.

FEDERAL OFFICE

Running for federal office—the United States Presidency, United States Senate, and United States House of Representatives—is a major effort, requiring significant political support, enormous funding, and a well-resourced team. The US Congress is our country's largest legislative body deliberating federal policy and appropriations. Members of the House of Representatives have two-year terms, and members of the US Senate have staggered six-year terms, meaning they are not all up for re-election at one time. As you look to your current federal leadership, many of those elected officials had been in local, county, or state service as they advanced through the levels of government.

As you think about your interests and ideas, match those with what level of service makes the most sense to achieve your positive goals. You may decide to make a difference on your board of education, city council, or zoning commission, and pursue a path of running locally. Alternatively, you may want to change state policy and run for the state legislature with a goal of serving in that body to impact your state's legislative, fiscal, or department policies.

From here on out, whether you are running in a county, city, town, village, or borough, we will call where you are running *the district*. No matter the level of government, every district boils down to voting precincts. That's the neighborhood location (often a school or library) where voters go to the polls and cast their ballots.

WHAT KIND OF RACE?

As you eye a seat you may want to run for, you will find each campaign will fall into one of these categories:

1. An open seat – When you run and there is not an incumbent (an incumbent is someone in office running again)
2. A challenge – When you run against an incumbent
3. A longshot – When you run against a *very* popular incumbent
4. A guarantee – Running unopposed and guaranteed to win the race

Not every race is a binary choice with a head-to-head against a candidate of the opposite party in the general election. Sometimes, you need to navigate getting support from your *own party* through a convention or primary process, which we will cover. And because there is never a dull moment in politics, you may consider running in a special election should a seat become vacant in the middle of an office holder's term. Of course, we have multi-candidate races (meaning candidates are running for many available seats), which we will discuss as well.

At this point you are taking inventory of your own achievements, no matter how small. You are being driven by *your Why*, and matching that passion with what level of government makes the most sense to you, focusing on a certain seat, and deciding what kind of campaign this would be: open, challenge, longshot, or a guarantee. You may not realize it yet, but you just laid the groundwork for your campaign.

LIFE OF
the Party

★ ★ ★

Major political parties have something you need—access to the ballot. One does not decide to just run for office and suddenly they are put before voters. There are a few ways to get onto the ballot, and we will discuss the importance of getting involved in your local political party just as you got involved in your community.

I hear the way people talk about major political parties, reminiscent of *The Wonderful Wizard of Oz* with some wizard behind a curtain pulling all the strings, single-handedly arranging every political move for everyone to see. Or they'll use the word "party" as if it's the name of an acquaintance with a checkered past: "So . . . did you hear what the Party did?"

The truth is, our electoral politics are decentralized and candidate-based, with political parties having waning influence over races. This has allowed for upsets in primaries and general elections, as major political parties are no longer as dominating as they were a generation ago. Parties were once machines with giants leading them: a monopoly with *total* control to leaders and money. Now, candidates and activist groups create much of the political infrastructure. Through the power of online organizing, accessible meetings, and a fragmented political and media landscape, the playing field has leveled, especially in local and state races.

Visit any political party meeting, and you'll see the magic of political parties is with the members: the people who do the organizing, increasingly with allied groups complementing efforts. When learning about your political party, seek out the members who are doing the work, and form relationships with them. You will also identify the influencers; important individuals who actually lead others in the group.

Visit any political party meeting, and you'll see the magic of political parties is with the members: the people who do the organizing, increasingly with allied groups complementing efforts.

LOCAL—AND COUNTY—PARTIES

The local party is there to help their own party's top-of-ticket—the mayor—and work to advance their message. Local parties meet regularly, often with committee meetings, and are engaged in person-to-person organizing following party bylaws. Because they are working in their own town, there is a great amount of pride in their work. For them, their efforts are personal as this is about their community. Many local groups will have outings, whether it's a monthly happy hour, pancakes and politics breakfast, or social dinner.

For my local party, our chairman would hold an annual coat drive where we would solicit winter coats and deliver them to our local shelter. It was a meaningful activity beyond politics that members would look forward to, and the receiving organization appreciated our local party's volunteerism.

The local party benefits from national and state programs, including technology and staffing that may be available. Still, local parties raise their own funds to support their efforts. Running for local office means you will get some level of help from your local party, whether they give contributions, guide you in your campaign, recruit volunteers, or simply offer that critical ballot line.

You may be surprised that some of the people you already met in the community are also involved in your local party, so you'll recognize familiar faces. Just as you did with your community, visit local party meetings, volunteer, and learn where your interests and skills match their needs and wants. You will find most of those involved in their local party have been there for many years and are looking for new ideas. If you feel frustrated by the lack of energy from your local party, don't give up or scream into the air. Instead, keep coming back, build relationships, and find others to support your local party. More than anything else, a local political party wants to win. By joining, you can help them do just that!

Just as you did with your community, visit local party meetings, volunteer, and learn where your interests and skills match their needs and wants.

STATE PARTY

Major state political parties fall under the national party and have their own staff and governing body—often called a state committee—who support local organizations of the same party. The state party leadership operates state conventions, keeps state party bylaws, and develops the state party platform. The state party supports the governor of the state, assuming they are of the same party. Further, state parties will have the voter file (literally the list of all voters) and programs available for candidates, as well as other resources to create a menu of tools for localities.

Keep in mind, just like federal candidates with the national party, the state party does not run candidates themselves. Candidates form their own committees separate from the state party. In a contested primary or convention process—when many candidates of the same party are running for an open position—the state party is setting the rules to conduct the process, which would include a nominating convention, but the party is not working for any one candidate. A candidate will have their own staff to work on their respective campaign, and they will liaise with the state party. Later, once the candidate earns the official party endorsement, the party will be more likely to offer tangible help for their endorsed candidate.

With so much expected of state parties, you may be surprised to know they are often longing for resources and attention—often squeezed between national politics, which grabs the headlines and donors; and local and state candidates who, rightfully so, are focused on their own campaigns. Stronger state parties, with dedicated leadership, more programs, and increased staffing would allow for a fully realized political apparatus with year-round organizing to benefit all localities, which we will discuss.

NATIONAL PARTY

The national party is run by a chair and a national governing body. Through messaging and fundraising, the national party supports the president of the United States, assuming they are of the same party. The party sets national functions like meetings, the presidential nominating schedule, national conventions, and maintains the party's national platform. They also fundraise enormous sums of money to keep the national party humming, investing in new technology and services that benefit state and local parties. The party works to communicate the message at a national level and helps create a favorable political environment for candidates of that same party.

When any party is out of power—whether it's the mayor or governor or president—even more is expected of the opposition party to be the attack dog and make the contrast to their opponents so candidates can shine on the campaign trail.

MINOR PARTIES

Besides the major political parties, Democratic and Republican, your district may have minor parties, which could represent partisanship (far left or far right), based on certain policy issues, or other circumstances which led that minor party to gain ballot access in your district. Beyond major and minor political parties, some candidates could even run as a write-in, meaning voters would need to write the candidate's name to cast a ballot for them. So, be mindful of the political environment you are in, what has worked for other candidates, and what parties have ballot access in your district.

CONVENTION

There are a few ways to get onto the ballot: conventions, signatures, and primaries. Chances are you will move through your political party for its endorsement, which can be formalized through a convention (that may be called a caucus or a meeting) where delegates will decide upon the endorsed candidate. It's likely you already met these delegates through getting involved politically, as the party's most faithful members are typically rewarded with being named a delegate. This type of endorsement event is a symbolic occasion showing you have the support of your party before the general election, and may include completing a questionnaire or interview to secure support. So, be sure to spend time forging relationships with political party members, as they will be influential in endorsement decisions.

At the convention, you will have a delegate nominate and second you, but beware there could be a floor nomination (when a delegate stands from the convention floor) putting someone else's name into the mix, so you never want to take anything for granted. Organizing for a convention means you will request the names and contact information of the delegates (the voting members) and draft a communications plan to ensure each one hears from you multiple times before delegates go into that endorsement event. This can include personal calls, a formal letter with your platform, and an email program outlining your priorities.

Going into the convention, ensure you have a commitment of support from each delegate. Candidates should always call delegates personally. Sometimes, all you need is a list of members, your phone, and time to be left alone. It goes a long way to show people that you take nothing for granted, and that you respect local party members and want to earn their support. Many times, if someone earns even a portion of support—for example, 15 percent of the voting members—they have the right to move on to a primary election; so even a segment of support at the convention could advance someone to a primary. Always understand the rules, as it changes depending on what your state laws are.

SIGNATURES

A candidate may earn ballot access by petitioning signatures from in-district voters, requiring a human-capital effort to collect more than enough signatures to qualify for the ballot. Candidates can recruit or hire people to go into the community seeking signatures for their candidacy from eligible voters according to local laws. You always want to have more signatures than needed, a rule of thumb being 10 percent more signatures than required, as some signatures may be thrown out for inaccuracies. An election authority will review your signatures consistent with state law and determine if you have the minimum number required to gain ballot access. This effort can be grueling because it's labor intensive, so if you go this route, be sure you are up for the challenge.

PRIMARY

Sometimes, more than one candidate from a party wants to run for the same office, and they secure ballot access through a qualifying endorsement event like a convention or through signatures. In a primary, the candidate asks voters for support over the same-party opponent before one advances to the general election. Primaries can be about intra-party fights or policy differences, but not always. Running a good primary election campaign is not unlike running a good general election campaign; the major difference is what segment of voters you are talking to.

Your state may have closed or open primaries, and that will be important to know for your primary campaign. A closed primary means only people registered to your party can vote, while an open primary means anyone registered can vote—so you can find innovative ways to reach all voters, not only your political party. The messaging in those respective primaries will differ if you are speaking to a wide electorate or just to those registered to your political party.

In a closed primary, the most partisan voters typically cast a ballot, so the question becomes who has more friends among the most motivated voters of the same political party? This requires strategy, a good understanding of the pulse of your political party, and deep connections among party leaders.

Some will enter into a primary to build name recognition for the future, or run on an issue they hope will gain traction. While some party members may not appreciate a primary effort, which could be viewed as wasting resources when they should be focusing on the general election, others may feel this is good for the party and helps strengthen candidates through a vigorous campaign.

Remember, when seeking ballot access, think of the avenues you could pursue: an endorsement event like a convention, qualifying signatures, or a primary. Should you have multiple candidates from your party vying for one seat, you need to win that primary election before you advance to the general election. Depending on your state, you may have a run-off election, where the top vote-getters of the same party compete against each other before the general election, as a way to clear the field with just the most viable candidates.

Of course, if you do not have a primary, and you've secured ballot access through your party, then you are *the* candidate for your party and are onto the general election! Once you are on that ballot, your placement could make a difference too. The ballot will begin with the largest federal races (if any are happening that year), then state, county, and local races. Your campaign is just one of many happening, and voters will be reviewing all the names on the ballot, if even for a moment. The ballot may include a question, called a referendum, and that may have an impact on your race—good or bad. Be aware of referendum questions, as it's a part of the conversation voters are having about this election. Some ballots have multiple pages, so when you know your exact ballot placement, tell people where they can find you. Keep in mind not every voter is partisan, meaning they only vote for one party. You may benefit from ticket-splitting, when a voter truly votes for the best candidate, and is not loyal to any one political party. We will talk more about the types of voters later.

While there still are barriers to entry in this political area, they are lower than before, and through understanding *your Why*, and early involvement in your district, you can grow a segment of support into broader appeal by securing support from an all-important political party. Your political party can give your campaign life, and *you* will then breathe new life into your political party.

DECISION
to Win

★ ★ ★

By now you have taken inventory of what drives you in this authentic journey to make a positive difference with a clear understanding of *your Why*. You have thought about what office you may run for, and know what kind of race it will be. You've met

★★★

When you make that decision to run, you're also making the decision to win.

the local political party and are thinking about how you will get on the ballot. Taken together, you're forming a solid basis that will prepare you for the campaign ahead.

When you make that decision to run, you're also making the decision to win. Be bold: Visualize the win, and then take every step toward that victory. You'll set yourself up for success by carrying out three important exercises as we decide to run, and decide to win:

- Your WIN (what I need) number
- SWOT (Strengths, Weaknesses, Opportunities, and Threats) analysis
- 360° awareness

WIN: WHAT I NEED

You don't need to know a lot about politics to know that the person with the most votes wins (except for the popular vote in a presidential election—but let's stay focused on you). That means for someone to have the most votes, they must have some level of popularity. While true, it's more mathematical than that. This is not complex math, but basic math: addition, subtraction, multiplication and at times, division. The first math equation you will determine is the expected voter turnout. In other words, how many people are going to vote in *this* election?

In order to determine this number, you'll want to compare apples to apples, so compare similar election years. This is a critically important step. You can view the prior election results on your states' secretary of state website and through local information on file. If you are running for a local board and your mayor is not up for election, pull the prior years when the races on the ballot looked *exactly* the same. In this case, you will focus on a local election when your mayor was not up for election.

Once you have the historical election data, gather the last three similar elections. Take the voter turnout for each similar election, and find the average. For example, if the last three similar elections' turnouts were 20,010, 19,000, and 19,300, you would add all three, then divide by three to get to 19,437. This is the number of people you can expect to vote in this year's election.

Think of WIN as *What I Need!* Your WIN number is the minimum number of votes you need to win an election. In most head-to-head races, you need 50 percent plus one to win. In this case, 50 percent plus one (always round up) of 19,437 is 9,720. That's how many votes you need to win.

$$20,010$$
$$19,000$$
$$+19,300$$
$$\overline{58,310}$$

$$\Rightarrow$$

$$58,310$$
$$\div \quad 3$$
$$\overline{19,437}$$

$$\left[\begin{array}{c} 50\% \text{ of} \\ 19,437 \end{array} \right] + 1 = \boxed{9,720}$$

This is your
WIN Number!

In local boards with multiple people running, you need to consider a multiple-person race, meaning you may need to earn only a fraction of votes to secure a seat on the board. For boards comprised of multiple elected officials, political party minority rules come into play, meaning for district-wide local offices, political parties may be *guaranteed* a certain number of seats, ensuring a level of balance so no one party has all the seats. If your party is guaranteed a seat because of political party minority representation, then you are also competing with people who share your political affiliation. In other words, you may need to be the top vote-getter among people in your same party to be elected onto the board. Let's take an example of a six-member board with minority representation of no more than four of any one political party.

R Candidate 1	6,510 votes	*WINNER*
R Candidate 2	6,489 votes	*WINNER*
R Candidate 3	6,221 votes	*WINNER*
R Candidate 4	5,989 votes	*WINNER*
R Candidate 5	5,780 votes	
D Candidate 6	5,771 votes	*WINNER*
D Candidate 7	5,658 votes	*WINNER*
D Candidate 8	5,490 votes	
GREEN Candidate 9	5,167 votes	

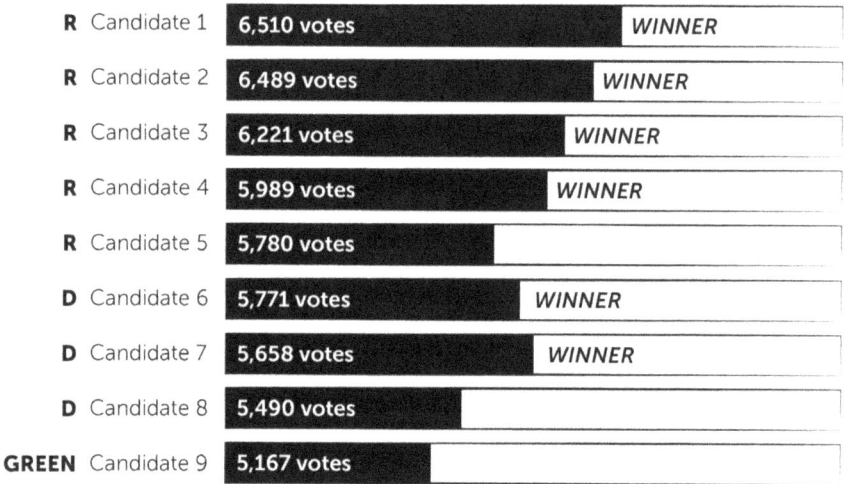

Seen here, the top four vote-getters from the Republican Party won, and the top two vote-getters from the Democratic Party won, based on the local rules around minority representation. Even though Candidate 5 had more votes than Candidates 6 and 7, there were already four people elected from that same party, so the top two vote-getters from another party were elected even though they received fewer votes than Candidate 5. This shows you minority party representation in practice.

Some states are moving to ranked choice voting, a way of casting a ballot where voters rank preferences in order, so if your first choice did not do well in the voting, your ballot continues to be counted for your next choice, and so on. The argument for this is that it will level the playing field and lessen the "us versus them" mentality of a campaign. You should know your district's election laws so you understand your local voting mechanism. Should your district vote by ranked choice voting, learn from colleagues in other states who have this voting process to determine what worked for them, which includes building coalitions and widespread popularity rather than contrast campaigning against a candidate.

360° AWARENESS

In politics, self-promotion is a necessary evil. In order to promote yourself, you need to know the messaging environment you are in. What are people saying out there? Your campaign must convey to voters who you are and what you hope to achieve. Social media has helped with this, as everyone nowadays is thinking of their personal brand, so you may have a sense of what your message is.

When I was a campaign manager, I could whip up a candidate bio and messaging points with ease. Yet, when I decided to run for office myself, I was no longer talking about someone else, but about *me*. It's so much easier to boast about someone else than it is about yourself. If you have helped others run, and are now thinking of running yourself, it entails a shift of focus to your own ideas for your district. This campaign is about your vision, so you need to be comfortable talking about yourself. Draft your bio, which should tell people who you are, and write down what your priorities would be in office. In other words, what did you want to achieve or create when you were thinking of *your Why?*

Now that you have determined your bio and priorities in office, let's elevate this concept because you are not just having a conversation with voters; you've got others out there talking *about* you, too. This message box exercise was designed for then-Governor Bill Clinton's first presidential campaign, and it has become a tried-and-true way for you to understand the message environment you are in before you knock on your first door.

Me on **ME**	Them on **THEM**
Me on **THEM**	Them on **ME**

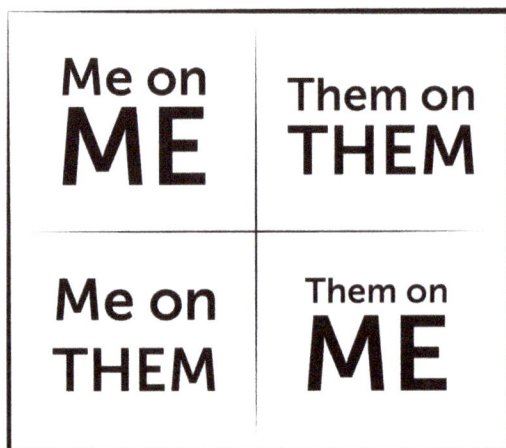

Draw a square and divide it into quadrants. Mark the upper-left square "Me on Me"; the upper-right square "Them on Them"; lower-left square "Me on Them"; and lower-right square "Them on Me."

The first box (Me on Me) is what you are going to be saying about yourself, your values, and vision. Keep these statements positive. Give people insight into who you are, why you are running, and your ideas for the district. This is not the place to mention your opponent. Just focus on *you*.

The next box (Them on Them) on the upper right is what your opponent is saying about themselves. Research their website, press statements, and social media so you are pulling information about what positive things they are self-reporting. This can be a challenge because you'll be critical of what they say about themselves, but stay focused and don't editorialize.

The bottom-left box (Me on Them) is for you to write what you are saying about them. What positions do they hold that are out of touch with the district? How will you push back against their claims? How do you want to define them in the race? Be sharp because they will be doing the same to you.

Finally, in the last box (Them on Me), think about what they are saying about you. They will emphasize your weaknesses, your inability to lead, or perhaps why your ideas are bad. Be critical of yourself so that you are ready for the harshest attacks.

Campaigns are not easy, and this message exercise illustrates the contrasts coming your way as you embark on this journey; as well as prepares you for how you will talk about yourself for the environment you are in.

SWOT ANALYSIS

Much like any new venture, you'll want to conduct a SWOT analysis for your candidacy. This is a strategic practice that will help you and your team identify strengths, weaknesses, opportunities, and threats. Drawing a box, you'll note the first column is helpful, while the second column is harmful. The first row is internal, and the second row is external, or public. When done correctly, this can help you position yourself in the campaign and be prepared for incoming attacks.

	Helpful	Harmful
Internal	*Strengths*	*Weaknesses*
External	*Opportunities*	*Threats*

Strengths are what give you an advantage over others. Always know your strengths, and accentuate them in your campaign. If you have excellent interpersonal skills and are great in one-on-one conversations, then get out there and prioritize door knocking and holding small gatherings.

Weaknesses are those elements that put you at a disadvantage; perhaps you just moved to the district and are unknown, or your daughter is getting married, and you will be out of the country for her destination wedding for a week before the election.

Opportunities are areas in your campaign you can use to your advantage; like new apartment buildings with hundreds of young people moving in, which your campaign thinks could be an untapped aid if they were to register and vote.

Threats are the elements in your campaign that could cause trouble; perhaps the candidate has admitted to the team that they have not paid business taxes in a few years, and that's about to go public.

Usually, strengths and weaknesses are internal considerations, while opportunities and threats are public. Once complete, try to match your strengths to opportunities; for example, you could host small conversations with those who recently moved to town if you do well in small group conversations, thereby registering new people to vote.

You also want to pair weaknesses with opportunities, bolstering your standing in the environment you are in. For example, a weakness could be that you are new to the district, while the opportunity is that you are unknown, and therefore can introduce—or brand—yourself to people for the first time. As for the weakness of the candidate being out of district for their daughter's wedding at the critical end-of-October period, make it known in advance that she's celebrating her daughter, and the campaign is having house parties every night phone banking to voters to ensure they don't lose any ground while the candidate celebrates with family. In that scenario, you actually may motivate *more* people to help volunteer than if the candidate were there.

When it comes to threats, make a plan. The candidate should get ahead of the forthcoming story, noting what taxes were missed and when; ideally with the announcement that it is paid back, or will be paid within a period of time. The candidate could talk with other small business owners who had similar struggles and discuss an economic agenda that helps working families and small businesses—because the candidate has lived through struggles, too. It's critical you vet your vulnerabilities and are upfront about any negative reports that may be revealed about you.

A great campaign is organized on the front end, with a clear understanding of your WIN number, full awareness of the

***

> **A great campaign is organized on the front end, with a clear understanding of your WIN number, full awareness of the messaging environment you are in, and a framework of your strengths, weaknesses, opportunities, and threats.**

messaging environment you are in, and a framework of your strengths, weaknesses, opportunities, and threats. You'll be standing on a strong foundation by knowing *your Why* and running these practical exercises for your candidacy.

For more on the decision to run, visit OrganizingtoWin.com

VISIBILITY
is Viability

★ ★ ★

R epresentative democracy is a bedrock American principle that, when fulfilled, guarantees every person a voice in this citizen government. When you have a diverse array of individuals making decisions about policy impacting families, you create a full view of the community and the needs of its people. Taken together, elected officials from different ideologies and backgrounds will generate more perspectives and ideas, which leads to greater learnings and discourse, whether it's on a board, town council, or state legislature. We see this in nearly every facet of life; you would not put the same kind of athlete in every position on the team, but rather, you would have an array of athletes with different strengths so that when taken together, the power is in the mix.

HISTORICALLY UNDERREPRESENTED

Given the time and resources it takes to run for office, it's not always a natural fit for a candidate to be someone juggling jobs, kids, and responsibilities—though that is who needs to be running for a fully representative government. We want everyone from every walk of life, and especially those who know the value of a hard-earned dollar.

Diverse perspectives require everyone's voice, and we want every person to participate. It means varying thoughts, socioeconomic backgrounds, religions, ages, races, ethnicities, LGBTQ+ community members, professions, small business owners, veterans, and people with a variety of abilities. We need more women in office and more young people from every zip code. For many, there is an intersectionality where candidates may have an identity reaching across communities.

As you look at your *own* representation, you may see elected boards, commissions, and legislative bodies—as well as executive positions—don't always look like the people they represent. The facts could not be clearer: Women make up half the population and outlive men, but only hold 32.9 percent of all state legislative seats. Among towns with a population over 30,000, only 26.8 percent have women mayors. Don't take my word for it; this is according to the Center for American Women in Politics.

There is so much data on this topic, but let's take a moment to review that Black Americans constitute 10 percent of state legislators, when they are about 15 percent of the national population, according to Pew Research Center. The Center for American Women in Politics reports that Black women are 5.4 percent of all state legislators, noting most of those gains were in the last decade. According to the National Association of Latino Elected and Appointed Officials, less than 2 percent of elected officials nationwide are Latino when they make up 18 percent of the population and are growing.

Members of the LGBTQ+ community only make up .25 percent (that's one-fourth of 1 percent) of elected officials, as reported by the LGBTQ+ Victory Institute. According to Gallup, 9.3 percent of US adults align themselves with the LGBTQ+ community, noting each younger generation is twice as likely as the previous generation to identify as LGBTQ+, and more than one in five Generation Z adults (those born between 1997 and 2012) identify with this community. The number of people who identify as LGBTQ+ is growing, particularly among young people, and they need to engage in politics. That's why I formed one of the first caucuses of the Connecticut Democratic Party, the LGBTQ+ Caucus, which is an organizing vehicle for more people to see themselves in the party and organize around policy. In just the first few years, we had doubled our LGBTQ+ representation at the local and state levels in Connecticut (we used many of the strategies I am going to share with you). That caucus became the blueprint for how communities could organize, and in the years since we formed many caucuses for groups adjacent to the party apparatus.

For women, it's not a question of winning, but of running. Some candidates may look at the job description and think, *I can do that.* Women, alternatively, may look at the skills required and think, *Do I have what it takes to do this well? Will I be able to assemble a team to pull this off?* We need to talk to women about getting involved, alleviating their concerns, and showing a path to win supported by a team. We need more women in office, and our persistence in asking them to run is important as we continue to strive toward a truly representative government. One of the ways women prepare to run locally is by attending training sessions that may be available, so search for training opportunities in your area.

I could go on, but these are real statistics showing a pattern of communities—often impacted by legislation and executive action—not involved in their government at a commensurate level. I hope you see the value in needing our government to represent people. For those who want to get involved but would make history as the first of an underrepresented group to hold the position, you may feel like you don't belong (once again with that imposter syndrome).

It's hard to think you belong when the very bodies you are hoping to enter do not look like you. *You need to know that you not only belong, but you are needed in that exact space.*

While running for office, I remember a voter said to me one day, "You must not be home a lot for the wife!" First, I was in my early twenties, and marriage wasn't even on my radar. "Ha-ha, no wife for me," I would deadpan. Was it my job to come out to every single person I met? Should I have said, "Actually, grab a chair, there's something I want to tell you." My age was clear by my apparent baby face, and because in American politics, your age is on every candidate profile; there's no escaping it. For members of the LGBTQ+ community, it may not be so apparent, and it's never a one-time occurrence. Being gay means you are always coming out in different spaces throughout life. For me, being gay was a part of my identity, and I bring my true self to everything I do, but I didn't lead with it because I wanted to talk about the work that needed to get done in town!

YOU'D BE THE FIRST

Having been elected to office in my early twenties, I was serving on boards and commissions with individuals three to four times my age—always in the political minority as well. At my first Planning & Zoning public hearing as a commissioner, I remember walking into our city hall auditorium to a stately mahogany table, with a name placard set out for each commissioner's seat, and adjacent to that was a small folding table, the kind you would set out at a backyard party and throw an ice bucket on. My name placard was at *that* folding table. Sure, it was a noticeable difference, but you cannot be bothered by such antics. It didn't matter what table they sat me at—voters elected me, and I wanted to get to work.

There are always challenges to running for office, but it's more pronounced if you are a barrier-breaking candidate. You need to assess if you have the financial security to take time off from work to run, have the support from your family, and have the courage to go for it. Because your networks may not be as developed as other more established and well-connected candidates, you could face barriers to securing funding and political support. Given this, some candidates are apprehensive and will wait for the *perfect* time. Politics is fluid, and the dynamics of the environment can change in an instant, so don't wait for the perfect moment. Make your moment when you are ready to participate. With hard work, involvement in your community, and an assertive approach to your political party, you'll soon be on your way to running for office.

★★★

Politics is fluid, and the dynamics of the environment can change in an instant, so don't wait for the perfect moment. Make your moment when you are ready to participate.

You are deciding to run because you care about something, and you want to do good in your community. As a candidate who may be the first, you will be ignored, underestimated, or sidelined. With your head down, just keep organizing. As others notice you are building an effort, some will try to discredit you because they realize you may be effective. Other times, there will be an effort, whether intentional or not, to have you become the sole authority on your own background, in effect marginalizing you as a token for the very community you are from, as if you can *only* speak for that community. Always bring your full identity with you, and don't let anyone take you from your purpose; *your Why*. This way, you won't be sidelined, silenced, or subjected to tokenism.

Being visible in your district is important, as people meeting you shows your viability, and suddenly, what started as a *different candidate* becomes a true contender. I have seen a surge of young people entering the political arena, and when they run for office they hear the words, "Well, if you won, you'd be the first."

New kinds of candidates are engaging in our politics, and they are winning. As a candidate from a historically underrepresented community, success does not mean that once you win, you close the door behind you, but rather you reach back and bring someone else along. Person by person, you can share your stories and help the next candidate, and their path may be more straightforward than yours.

In our society, being the first to do something is revered, but I challenge you that the accomplishment is not being the first in making history—it's ensuring you are making progress, and working to bring others into this arena so you are not the last.

HELLO,
Candidate

★ ★ ★

Running for office is an entrepreneurial effort as you are build-ing an organization from scratch. This requires a vision, human capital, resources, and a goal-oriented plan to meet benchmarks

Making your announcement official and establishing your campaign with a strong team—from your kitchen cabinet to staff and volunteers—will set you up for success as the days on the campaign trail intensify.

with a timeline. Being a candidate means being an innovator; you are literally starting a new enterprise. It demands being creative, resourceful, disciplined, and motivated to lead through pressures and setbacks. Making your announcement official and establishing your campaign with a strong team—from your kitchen cabinet to staff and volunteers—will set you up for success as the days on the campaign trail intensify.

COMMITTEE TYPE

When you decide to run for office, one of the decisions you will make early on is what kind of committee you will have:

- Candidate Committee – The funds you raise go to support your candidacy, and only your candidacy. This is where you have a dedicated bank account, and when someone makes a contribution, it goes to benefit your campaign. An example of this would be a mayoral campaign where you have your own committee with a treasurer.
- Slate Committee – You run with several candidates, as a collaborative team. This means you all share a treasurer, and when someone makes a contribution, it goes to benefit everyone on the slate. How you determine the distribution of funds is a group decision as you are all running together as a unit. An example of this would be people of the same party running as a slate for the board of education in town.
- Party Committee – Oftentimes for local office, you may run through your local political party, where you use their infrastructure and treasurer. Party leadership will decide how much to budget for your campaign, and they can be convinced to invest more if you demonstrate you are fundraising on behalf of the party and working hard to win. An example of this would be elected finance board members

or the sole library director role, who run their campaigns through the local party. For first-time candidates, this may be a good place to start.

KITCHEN CABINET

A "kitchen cabinet" is a political term for a trusted group of people, usually fewer than ten, who will be a part of confidential conversations around your candidacy. A good team may have someone who has successfully run themselves, those who have a sense of the district, and respected community members. At some point in the campaign, you need people who will course correct and speak up when things are not going well, so having trusted and competent people will be beneficial. Examples of a good kitchen cabinet member include:

- A friend who plans to lead volunteer efforts
- A subject matter expert who helps with policy papers
- Someone who held the position before you
- A supportive local business owner
- A spouse who will serve as a surrogate (A surrogate is a person who goes out into the community with the authority to speak on behalf of the candidate.)

A kitchen cabinet that meets regularly will be familiar with each other's working styles once the campaign gets rolling. The cabinet should be a safe place to experiment with ideas, communications, and monitor the campaign step by step. Kitchen cabinets used to literally meet around the kitchen table in the candidate's house, but now your cabinet can be a texting thread, an email chain, or a virtual meeting.

CAMPAIGN TEAM

Beyond the kitchen cabinet, you need people to help with defined roles. When meeting with people who want to join your team as staff or volunteers, consider asking these questions:

- What other campaigns have you worked on?
- What was your favorite part of that campaign? Your least favorite?
- Are you going to be working on other campaigns at the same time as mine?
- Have you lost a campaign? What lessons did you learn?
- What do you know about the district I am running in?
- Why do you want to work for me on this race?

When hiring, consider bringing on people who know your district well. Otherwise, be prepared for someone with the skillset who will need to learn the culture of your district: the traditions, people, and way of life. Every campaign size is different, but you'll be bringing people on for various roles including:

- Campaign Manager – The overall supervisor and driver of the campaign, who will ensure the campaign stays focused, as well as a liaison to the candidate. We'll talk even more about the campaign manager role later.
- Finance Director – Leads the finance efforts to raise funds and track all campaign spending.
- Treasurer – Legally responsible for all financial dealings and campaign finance reports. They work with the finance director and even a day-to-day bookkeeper.
- Political Director – For larger races, they will coordinate the political relationships with elected and party officials.

- Field Director – Oversees the field, or voter-contact, operation. Under this role could be several coordinators who have assigned geographic areas.
- Volunteer Coordinator – Works closely with the field director to ensure the campaign is recruiting and engaging volunteers. On smaller campaigns, this can be the field director.
- Communications Director – Leads all communication efforts to keep the candidate present in all forms of media, and is the point of contact for the press.
- Press Secretary – Supports the communications director and deals directly with the campaign's social media accounts, press releases, and related needs.
- Operations Director – Working with the treasurer, and possibly a bookkeeper, they will keep a record of all contracts and records, and oversee the operations of headquarters. In a small campaign, this might be the campaign manager.
- Bookkeeper – Closely manages the campaign ledger: money in and out, with everything tracked.
- Scheduler – Maintains the schedule for the candidate and campaign. On smaller campaigns, this can be the campaign manager or trusted person to the candidate.
- Interns – Your campaign can welcome newcomers who want to gain experience on a regular basis as part of an intern program. They can be at-large or for a specific issue area. We will talk more about interns later.

Of course, this can be scaled where positions are combined or even increased by adding deputies under each director. It's important to have legal help throughout the campaign to ensure you follow all campaign finance laws. Your treasurer should be following all guidelines, and when in doubt, reach out to your jurisdiction's campaign authority to ensure you are acting appropriately.

The structure of your organization can vary based on size. An organizational chart could look like this:

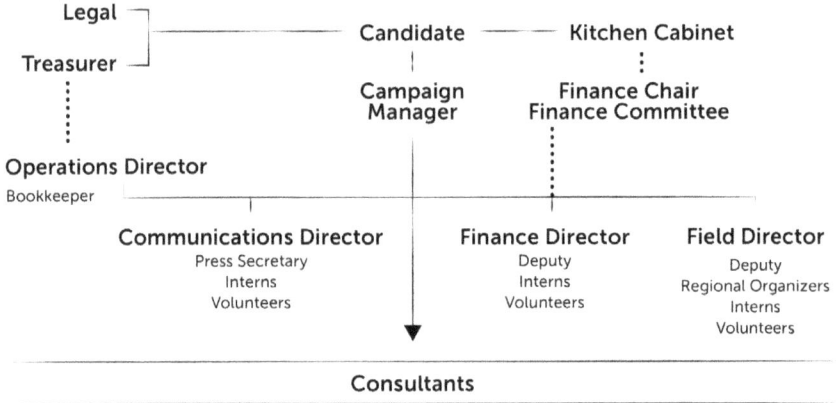

YOUR GO-TO LIST

This effort will require you to reach out to lots of people for support, so think through groups of people beyond your kitchen cabinet and put them in one uniform list, collecting mailing addresses, cell numbers, and emails. Think of people associated with these groups you are a part of:

- Family
- Friends
- Neighbors
- Co-workers
- Professional associations
- Political, labor, and advocacy groups
- Social, church, and community organizations
- Parents of your children's activities and teams
- Affinities like fellow nurses, teachers, fraternities, or small business owners

- Places you frequent and the people you see there, like a café, gym, or shop
- For a barrier-breaking candidate, leaders in that very community

You may be surprised with the list you create, spanning a wide range of people. Don't limit yourself to only people who live in your district; anyone can volunteer, and almost anyone can donate.

ARE YOU READY?

As the saying goes, failing to plan is planning to fail. Before you announce your candidacy, review the topics we've covered and ask yourself these questions:

- What do I know about my district?
- What do I want to improve or enhance?
- What is *my Why*?
- What elected seat best matches my interests?
- What kind of race will this be? (Open, challenge, longshot, or a guarantee.)
- Will I file my own committee, run with a slate, or part of a local party?
- Do I have a primary, or am I onto the general election?
- How will I seek a party endorsement to get on the ballot?
- Do I have a 360-degree view of what I will say about myself, what I would say against an opponent, what that opponent will say about themselves, and what they will say about me?
- Did I run a Strengths, Weakness, Opportunities, and Threats analysis?
- Have I analyzed past voter turnout in this kind of race?
- Did I set my WIN number?

- Have I set aside time to campaign every day?
- Do I have a core group for a kitchen cabinet?
- Have I brought on a campaign manager?
- Do I have a treasurer?
- Who am I leaning on for legal advice?
- Have I identified individuals who can help work or volunteer on the campaign?
- Have I gathered all the people I know for a go-to list?

ANNOUNCING YOUR CANDIDACY

The day has come to start your campaign, and you will need to announce and file paperwork consistent with local or state rules. Visiting your town clerk or election authority's office, you will learn what exactly you need to file. You will need a campaign treasurer, a trusted person who will oversee the funds. With your own

Always be sure to define yourself before your opponent can define you.

committee, you will need a dedicated bank account, an employer identification number, and all records to be kept by your treasurer.

A good announcement can include an in-person event surrounded by supporters, especially for a more senior-level position like a mayor's seat. For legislative seats, you could announce online using an email, or with a short video of you talking to the camera about why you are running. On the morning of your announcement, your social media and press release should launch at the same time.

Having a working website, contribution page with a processing vendor, press release, social media channels, and email blast ready to go takes coordination, but your campaign will be better for it.

A good announcement rollout will tell voters who you are. *Always be sure to define yourself before your opponent can define you.* Without a plan going into an announcement, no one will notice, and you will have blown the first opportunity to make your candidacy known. As you announce your candidacy, ensure you have the most critical pieces in place:

- Candidacy paperwork filed in the proper office
- A working bank account, verified by your treasurer
- An employer identification number
- A press release for local press outlets
- Your bio
- A photo of you
- A working website with contribution page
- Social media channels created
- A short video for social media use
- Contracts signed and on file
- Campaign insurance secured

IT'S OFFICIAL

Be proud that you've come this far on your journey. You're announcing a run for public office in your district by showing up and organizing. You wanted to get involved, and you are engaging in a meaningful way, leading you to this moment.

You may be thinking about *all the other things* you need to get done in this campaign. There will be a lot battling for your attention, so you need to abandon the idea you will ever be fully caught up on that to-do list of yours. Every day there will be many things to get done, and no matter how many tasks you are juggling, you can break down every campaign into four areas:

- Me (the candidate)
- Mobilization
- Money
- Message

We have talked about you, the candidate. Next, we will discuss the critical areas of a campaign: a field effort with volunteers (mobilization), fundraising (money), and communications (message). These pieces are all interconnected as the clock ticks toward your election; and we do not get any more time in this campaign. As I told you, we are going to make your campaign special, one that people will remember, and one that will benefit our democracy.

We've got a lot to cover, so let's keep going, candidate.

PART II

MOBILIZATION, MONEY, & MESSAGE

UNIVERSE
of Data

★ ★ ★

After managing that initial mayoral campaign in my home-town, I did what any reasonable person in their twenties at the height of a recession would do: I quit a stable job in New York and immersed myself in political volunteerism at home. I would attend community gatherings, make friends with those who worked for elected officials, run for office myself, and start managing local and state campaigns. I learned quickly that all good campaigns had one thing in common: *data*. In every campaign, behind piles of lawn signs and boxes of printed literature, is a treasure-trove of data.

Remember when I said the best *candidate* does not always win? Sometimes, the campaign can be so well organized that it can offer cover to a candidate who is still learning how to excel in this space. We are going to talk about the science of campaigning; the tactics that, if utilized, will ensure your campaign is reaching voters, raising funds, and communicating your message. A voter may not see *every single thing* your campaign releases, but they could catch a glimpse of an ad, hear of your candidacy from others, or see you from a distance at an event.

VOTER FILE

Investments in technology by national parties have allowed campaigns to access powerful voter databases that provide valuable information. What you do with that data is the science behind your campaign, and it will make all the difference as you keep it up to date.

If you are running with a major political party, you can gain access to their official voter file, which is a data system offering public information like a voter's name, address, age, basic democratic information, party affiliation, voting history (when they voted, not how they voted), and scores. A score is a rating assigned to you based on information analyzed. So, let's say you are a Democratic candidate; you'll find there is a score for the likelihood a voter will support a Democratic candidate for national office and state office, and even how likely they are to support an array of issues, like gun violence prevention legislation. When I was first getting involved, I thought the idea of scores seemed overreaching, but a good campaign needs to *know something* about their voters, and national parties are building this data for your benefit to make sound judgements about who to speak to in your campaign. While a score is not always perfect, it will suggest voters' behavior in general or with relation to a specific issue.

For those on a shoestring budget, you can talk with your local election official for their list of voters, which they can provide without a cost (or a nominal fee, if they are printing it for you). This will give you basic information about voters and will still be helpful in your targeting.

TARGETING VOTERS

Don't assume you know your district simply because you live there. With your team, dig into the data and learn about the district's demographics and voter registration. There are a lot of voters to talk to, and you can break them down into several segments:

- Base Democrats – Historically vote in every election, and always vote for the Democratic candidate
- Lean Democrats – Usually vote for the Democratic candidate in elections
- Unaffiliated or Non-Major Party Voters – Voters not registered with a major party
- Lean Republicans – Usually vote for the Republican candidate in elections
- Base Republicans – Historically vote in every election, and always vote for the Republican candidate

For your race, you are going to create your own target groups of voters whose support you will strive to earn:

- Base – You can rely on these prime voters to support you; they may be of the same political party, share your ideology, or belong to a group that you assume will be a strong supporter—and they always vote in your kind of election! This is your foundation of support.
- Persuasion – These voters are not guaranteed to vote for you, so you need to speak with them in order to earn their support. They often cast a ballot in an election like yours but need to be persuaded to vote for *you.*
- Motivation – This is the segment of voters who rarely vote in local or state races but always do in presidential-year races. Often called low-propensity voters, these presidential-year voters cast a ballot every four years in the biggest elections. We'll talk more about this group later and how to inspire them to vote.

- Unregistered – These are people you come across who are excited to support you, but they are not even registered to vote. These people offer potential to expand the electorate.

Whenever you can, add new voters, which in large amounts can be surprisingly disruptive to your opponent's understanding of the electorate.

FIELD PLAN

Remember your WIN number, the number you need to reach on Election Day? Well, this voter list you created is going to provide you ways to get to that WIN number. Too often, people think running for office requires talking to *every single person* in the district, but that is far from the truth for a campaign with a set amount of time to organize.

Remember, different elections will command varying levels of turnout; in other words, how many people vote. The largest turnout will always be a presidential election. State elections, like a gubernatorial contest, will usually have lower turnout than a presidential election, and local elections will reflect the smallest turnout. Should that local election be a special election, like when a vacancy occurs mid-term, turnout will be abysmal. Realizing this, it means that every vote really *does* count. After every election, I know a candidate who won (or lost) by literally a handful of votes.

Let's break it down. Your district will have a lot of voters. But, not all of them vote in every election. You will want to look at the elections that match your current election—exactly as we did with your WIN number—meaning comparing the race you are in

	ALWAYS VOTE DEMOCRATIC	SWING VOTERS	ALWAYS VOTE REPUBLICAN
ALWAYS VOTE	DEMOCRATIC BASE	PERSUASION TIER 1	REPUBLICAN BASE
SOMETIMES VOTE	DEMOCRATIC GOTV	PERSUASION TIER 2	REPUBLICAN GOTV
NEVER VOTE	MOTIVATE	PERSUASION TIER 3 & MOTIVATE	MOTIVATE

with the *exact type* of election in your district in the past. So, if you are running for mayor, you are going to look at numbers from previous mayoral campaigns in your district. Pull those voters who cast a ballot in local elections like the one you are in, and that will give you the electorate that is likely to vote in *this* local election.

Using that list of local election voters, you'll want to experiment with the data to find how you can get to that WIN number, which in a head-to-head match-up is 50 percent plus one. You would be right to start by removing the staunchest members of the *other* party, further targeting your base voters and persuasion voters. As we've outlined, your base voters are those who vote in your exact election, and whose scores show they vote for your political party. In other words, they vote, *and* they vote for your party. You will need to talk to the persuasion voters, those who vote in your exact election, but whose scores show they are not always a supporter of your political party. Those voters—base and persuasion—are going to offer you the clearest path to your WIN number, ensuring your election.

Take a look at this street in your district to understand why you need to be intentional with outreach. What do you see?

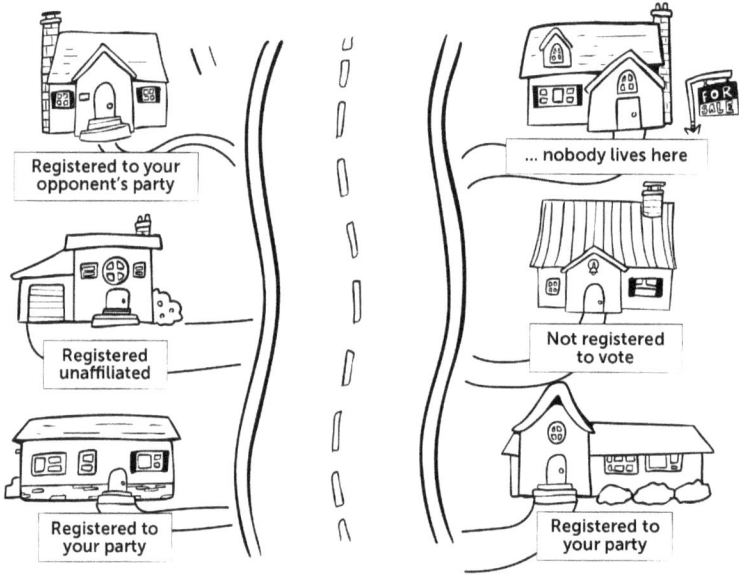

As a campaign with a goal to win in a defined amount of time and with limited resources, you must prioritize outreach to your targeted voters. Even the most exuberant candidates will eventually

---

As a campaign with a goal to win in a defined amount of time and with limited resources, you must prioritize outreach to your targeted voters.

---

realize that it's impossible to talk to *every* voter. Let's say you have four months until Election Day, and you think you can door knock ninety minutes every day (knowing you will miss some days), and you can get to thirty doors an hour; that's forty-five houses a day. This, of course, varies by district—from city buildings to country roads. Still, with these figures, in a week, you're at about three hundred houses. Over a month, it's about fifteen hundred doors, and over that four-month span, it's just over six thousand doors attempted. While that is incredible, it *still* may not be enough to reach your WIN number.

ONE PARTY DOMINANT

If you are in a race where your political party dominates your district, and the base voters *alone* guarantee your win, then you can likely focus on base voters, and you'll be well on your way to winning. In fact, in that scenario, your challenge will be the primary election and not the general election. In this kind of race, you will appeal and get the support of those in your party to win.

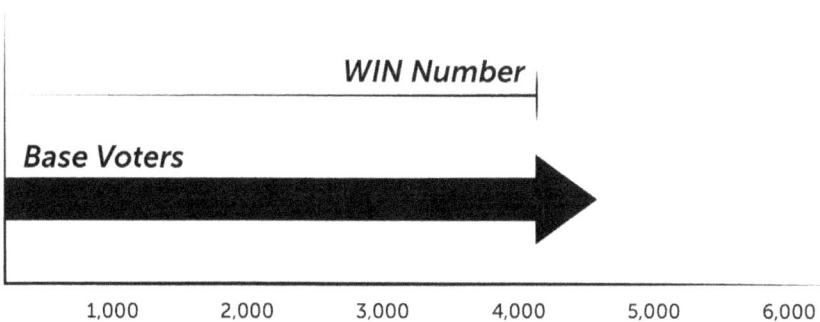

PURPLE DISTRICT

For many districts, you will need a combination of base and persuasion voters to win your election. This is where your hard work will pay off through a good campaign. In this case, your campaign may need to prioritize the persuadable voters so you are talking to the people who will vote but need convincing about your candidacy.

If your campaign does this, then your local party can compliment efforts by talking to base voters knowing they will likely vote for you.

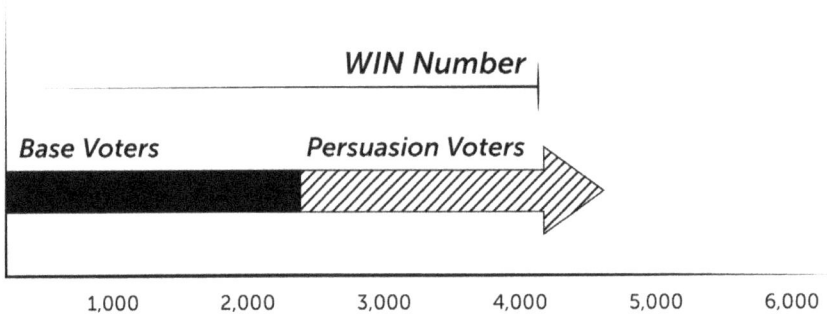

TOUGH RACES

Even after targeting using the available data, you may be short of your number. This means that even with base and persuasion voters, you *still* do not have enough support to win. Some districts are tough, in part because of political gerrymandering, the practice of drawing districts to benefit one party. These are the tough races where more work needs to be done to get to that WIN number. You must bring more people out to vote, including motivation voters, and talk about the good you will do when in office though meaningful year-round organizing, which we will discuss.

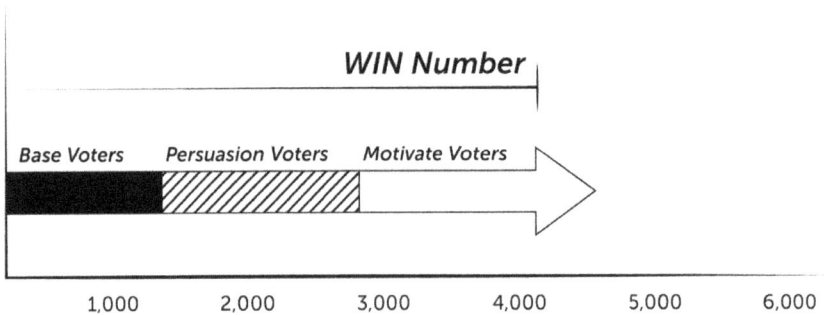

Here are a few ideas for how to inspire those motivation voters who seem to skip the elections that have the greatest impact on their lives—local elections:

- Have volunteers canvass them and discuss how important this election is.
- Mail a postcard including what's at stake, and have a volunteer call them to follow up.
- Print a list and have key volunteers review it for friends and family, thereby using a relationship model where people hear from friends nudging them to vote in this election.
- Since these voters are presidential-year voters, volunteers can connect federal action (or inaction) to local needs, and how important this race is because of the state of national politics.
- Informing people the election will be close—and that their vote could make the difference—will resonate with voters.

When thinking of your district, be mindful that political attitudes can change as people move in and out of the district, so they are not static; they are ever-changing, and you need to keep your finger on the pulse of the district.

LEVERAGE INFLUENTIAL GROUPS

Interest-based groups, affinity organizations, indivisible chapters, and unions can be influential in a campaign, if those members choose to engage in the race. Naturally, there can be overlap between members of that external organization and your local party because there are similarities in the values of your party and that group. When you run for office, anyone can door knock for you, so engaging with these groups will be helpful. These groups can offer expertise on policy positions, bring awareness to your candidacy, and introduce new people to your campaign. Find organizations that have a natural complement with your candidacy, whether it's supporting union households, environmental policies, faith based efforts, or civil rights, and get those members involved in your campaign by forming relationships with them. Since your values are aligned, they'll be helping your race, and advancing issues they care about.

VOTER REGISTRATION

Seek opportunities to expand the political landscape by registering more people to vote. A mentor of mine, longtime Connecticut Democratic Party Chairwoman Nancy DiNardo, would always ask people if they were registered to vote because she knew every single person makes a difference in a campaign. Never taking anyone for granted, she would tell me how she kept voter registration forms on her, so no matter where she may be—from a political event to the grocery store—she could register someone to vote. Now, with technology, people can register to vote online with ease.

Check your local and state rules around voter registration, and always have voter registration forms or the appropriate website on hand to register people. Further, your campaign can have volunteers at community events to simply ask if people are registered to vote and have them complete the process to register.

Your campaign can track new voters through the local registrar of voters office, or through your party's voter database. The information will have a delay in being entered, but at some point those new voters will be added into each system. Regularly, take those new voters and put them in two categories: those in your political party and unaffiliated voters (meaning they did not register with any political party):

- For those who belong to your party, send a letter welcoming them and inviting them to an upcoming event or meeting with your political party.
- For those who recently registered as unaffiliated (meaning no political party), send them a letter or a postcard about what is on the ballot this year, and why it's important to vote.

Base and persuasion voters are your top priority, but should you have the time and funds, or simply need to expand the electorate to get to your WIN number, these techniques offer paths to reach motivation voters, all while registering more people to vote. Combined, you could change the political landscape by adding new voters and getting low propensity voters (those who do not vote regularly) to cast a ballot. Your opponent may not know just how many people you are registering until it's too late for them to develop their own voter registration plans.

Over the course of your campaign, you are speaking, in layered ways, with targeted individuals based on the data you have. These groups—whether base, persuasion, motivation, or newly registered voters—make up your universe. And if all goes according to plan, that universe will be 50 percent plus one (or greater) of the electorate for a head-to-head race. Your campaign will be totally focused on talking, again and again, to your universe with the goal of hitting your WIN number.

REACHING
Voters

★ ★ ★

At this point, you have made the decision to run (and win), have a core team in place, determined your WIN number, and formed your universe of voters. Your campaign has taken shape, and it's time to speak to that universe of voters: shake hands, meet people where they are, and listen to their concerns. Meeting people where they are means speaking to them *physically* where they are: on a doorstep, at an event, online; and *emotionally* where they are: their perceptions, feelings, and frustrations. In fact, good campaigning is more listening, and less talking. Before we go out there and meet voters, remember we are in a fast-paced society, and people seem to be getting busier, don't they? Placing a candidate in front of them—and getting a positive reaction—takes work, but it will make all the difference to winning your race.

When you are carrying out voter outreach, tune out all the other things you need to do, personal, professional, or political. You must stay focused on that voter in front of you because in that moment, *that's* the most important element of your campaign. In fact, you would be wise to remember something about that voter so when you speak with them again, you continue to develop the relationship. Was their child going off to college? Were they doing some work on the house? Did they just join an organization in town? Good campaigns will use multiple ways to speak to voters again and again, creating a synergy across all their efforts. This approach will make a difference in building a bond between you and the voter. Importantly, you need to ask them for their support. Never assume that a nice conversation will lead to you securing a vote—you must ask for each vote. Let's review the ways you can reach voters.

***

Never assume that a nice conversation will lead to you securing a vote—you must ask for each vote.

PHONE BANKING

Let's say you have a volunteer who is willing to talk to voters but wants to stay at headquarters. In this case, phone banking is a good option for them. You will provide them with a brief script, which will have talking points to read about your campaign, ensuring the most nervous volunteer can read through it. They can even practice with another volunteer to become familiar with the script before they start calling. You will provide them the information for who exactly to call using the universe established. You may consider having senior citizens call fellow seniors or have people call into their own precincts, so they are talking with neighbors. As with all voter outreach, you can have lists printed or electronically available.

There are virtual programs for a fee that can help, so talk to your local and state political party for suggestions. These tools aim to decrease the amount of time one spends waiting for a voter to answer the phone. The volunteer simply uses a laptop or tablet to pull up a voter list, one voter at a time with their name, basic information, and phone number. The program is synced with a phone, and they will call voter to voter. As they conclude the call and mark it complete, the next voter will answer. This happens because as they are wrapping up one call, the program is calling out to many households, dropping calls in the event no one answers, and only connecting volunteers to live individuals. By doing this, they can reach more voters than they ever could through old-fashioned paper sheets, living in voicemails and wrong numbers. The first time I used this, I thought I was a professional call center of one!

When I first ran for local office, my mom wanted to help, so from her own kitchen table, she called one thousand senior citizens in town, letting them know, "I'm Jimmy Tickey's mom." I am not quite sure how much of my talking points she relayed, but she didn't need to—she was the candidate's mom calling fellow senior citizens. On Election Day, voters would happily approach me, hold my arm, and say, "I chatted with your mom."

TEXTING

You are probably familiar with national texts, often from a candidate you have never heard of, and are left wondering how you even got on their list. Texting is used widely for national races and less so on local ones. There are paid texting programs that allow volunteers to use a service to text directly with voters, which can be helpful in races like yours. This could be a message asking for a vote, but even better is one asking for engagement. If used correctly, you can learn something about your voters. Say, for example, months out from the election, you text voters asking what's important to them and include options like fixing the streets, improving schools, and reinvigorating downtown. Those answers provide data that your campaign can use, adding it into your database. Say you texted a voter and there is a response that reinvigorating downtown is their top issue. Later, when your campaign has a mailing on your plan to revitalize downtown storefronts, you include this voter (and others like them) who reported this was their top issue. These voters can be marked with a code so they are easy to pull and speak to in the future. Text banking (like phone banking) is useful for those voters who would never answer a call and may be hard to reach, particularly young people. When campaigning, include texting as it's a sure way to get in front of a voter.

MAILINGS

Printed mailings have a short life, often from the voter's mailbox to their trash, but are a key component of a political campaign. If you are lucky, your mailing may sit on the kitchen table for a few days before being swept up. With that in mind, these important components of your campaign should have your picture, logo, slogan, and the date of Election Day, including early voting details. Additional content may be added, but you do not want to overwhelm the piece with text. Your first piece of mail should introduce yourself to voters, while later pieces should convey stances on issues using plain language. This is not a policy paper—this is a mailer to grab people's attention with a few points, so don't make it complicated.

Further, targeted mailers can be sent to a segment of the list, called microtargeting. For example, your announcement to renovate the senior center can be sent to those sixty-five years and older, and perhaps your plan to address flooding in a specific precinct in your district will be sent to that geographic area. Microtargeting in this way can be powerful and, over time, will create multiple layered communications.

LETTERS TO THE EDITOR

While the candidate is welcome to pen their own letter to the local paper, it's more impactful to have someone not associated with the campaign write a letter. Ideally, that letter should hit at a time when the topic is most relevant. Say, for example, you release a senior-tax abatement plan. That could be amplified by seniors writing letters to the editor and a mail piece going out to seniors about the plan in sequential order, keeping the focus on this issue for an extended period of time.

Having notable community members pen a letter is desirable as they may be well known, thereby validating your campaign. This could include business owners, respected members of the community, those involved in civic groups, or someone who has been in office before. Typically those in leadership positions of a nonprofit 501(c)3 will not be able to do so given their nonprofit status, but you can find volunteers who are not in the leadership of those organizations.

HOUSE PARTIES

"You should have a coffee-and," my parents said when I first ran for local office. What is a coffee-and? Turns out, it's a small house gathering where some of your friends and supporters host a coffee (or drinks with snacks), and their task is to get their neighbors to attend. Think of it as a meet-and-greet friendraiser (not fundraiser) where you pull together small groups, getting community members to engage in dialogue in a personal setting.

Your campaign should lay out who will host these events and then, using your universe, pull targeted voters in the area of each house gathering. Combined with the hosts inviting neighbors and your campaign sending it to others, you've created a segment of your list to communicate for this event. Hold these events later in the day, when you can no longer door knock, and advertise it for one hour so the expectation is set for the duration of the event. You'll be pleasantly surprised by the result, as it's a nice way to get to know neighbors, secure lawn sign locations, and practice public speaking in small groups. Your campaign can ask each attendee if they would be willing to host a similar gathering of people among their own networks (think book clubs, church groups, and Parent Teacher Associations).

POSTCARDS

While a more passive tool, if you have a volunteer who does not want to phonebank, and cannot walk door to door, then put them to work with other efforts like a postcard program. Remember when we were targeting your universe? We spoke about those motivation voters who need some inspiration to vote in a local election. Develop a postcard program, so volunteers can write a note and address it to targeted people like motivation voters as a first step toward getting them to vote.

LAWN SIGNS

Your campaign will place lawn signs at the homes and businesses of people who support you. In rural and agricultural areas, larger signs are put out showing support since homes are more spread out. Be sure to use the same graphic across all of your signs for maximum consistency, and be mindful if there is a rule-of-thumb in your district about when lawn signs should go out.

On my first campaign, I would hop in the car with friends, and we drove my lawn signs all over town. As a first-time candidate, I felt like if I did not have more lawn signs than my opponents, I would never win. I now realize lawn signs show visual support, but *lawn signs don't vote*. Not to mention, opponents will likely steal some of your signs, so please do not obsess over the lawn sign games. On my largest lawn signs, I would drop off a fall mum plant to beautify the sign location, and the hosting family appreciated the gesture.

GROUP VISIBILITY

You can't knock on doors at 7:30 a.m., but you can have a group of volunteers waving your signs on a sidewalk or busy intersection as people commute, or at the local train station. While this is a passive (and not targeted) approach, this will get folks honking horns and cheering you on, and it's exciting for volunteers.

ROBOCALLS

Check local rules, but in many areas you can send a recorded message to homes that will leave a voicemail with the proper legal attributions (this is "paid for by" information). This can be a well-known public figure endorsing you, or even a direct message from the candidate to remind the voter when Election Day is. While not personal, they are inexpensive and a way to send a message to voters quickly.

LIT DROPS

Rather than talking to voters, volunteers go door to door and drop off information about your candidacy reminding them to vote. Sometimes this is done during the final days of the campaign. While it's still targeted to who you need to get out and vote, you are not engaging in conversation. This is a good activity for students and inexperienced campaigners to go out in pairs and still beneficial for a campaign.

SWAG

Mindful of the scale of your campaign, your team may be interested in having your logo printed on shirts, pins, bumper stickers, and other merchandise. Volunteers can sport your swag around town, further increasing public awareness of your campaign.

With repeated contacts with voters, people will not only recognize you, but your presence will evoke a feeling when they see you. You've begun to build a brand for yourself.

When all these techniques are used together, you will build name identification and create greater awareness about your candidacy. With repeated contacts with voters, people will not only recognize you, but your presence will evoke a feeling when they see you. You've begun to build a brand for yourself.

What am I missing? That's right, the most effective campaign technique: door knocking.

COMFORTABLE
Shoes

★ ★ ★

D oor knocking is the picturesque American effort to have a clipboard in hand and go door to door in a neighborhood. You'll be having conversations with people one by one, block by block, winning over a district through meaningful conversations as the breeze flows through your hair, birds sing to you, and people give you a thumbs-up as you stroll down their street. The idea of it is romanticized more than the actual practice of it. In reality, you'll be walking up a hill, unable to find the number of the house you are looking for, sweating on a hot summer day as cars are buzzing by, knowing your friends are at brunch and you are left wondering . . . *Why am I doing this to myself?*

You are in essence knocking on the doors of strangers. People are busier than ever with their noses in their phones, and a ring at the doorbell isn't as welcome as it used to be. We have grown accustomed to even our meals and packages being dropped off quietly, and the slightest motion of a leaf blowing in the wind triggers the motion doorbell. So, to see a stranger approach the doorstep can leave people feeling leery. But the truth is, when you engage people in conversation they *are* more likely to be interested in the issues, and in the upcoming election.

Door knocking is an opportunity for you to look a voter in their eyes and welcome their participation in public policy, and there is no better way than it coming from the candidate at the voter's doorstep. Once you start door knocking, you will see why this community-building effort can make all the difference. Voters will remember a connection with a candidate, and more than what you said, *they will remember how you made them feel.*

Door knocking is an opportunity for you to look a voter in their eyes and welcome their participation in public policy, and there is no better way than it coming from the candidate at the voter's doorstep.

Voters view a candidate in two ways: first, were you *likable*, and second, were you *capable*? Being likable means did they trust you and find you warm? People don't care what you know until they know that you care. Then, the other piece is more about authority; did you have some level of perceived competence and reliability? So, on their doorstep were you just popping by and dropping off information? Or did you ask if they had thoughts about the district? Did you explain your plan as to how you will improve quality of life? Did you *listen* to them and hear their thoughts?

One time, while I was door knocking with a candidate, the candidate mentioned the downed tree at the end of the street to the voter. The tree was on town property, and the tree brush was impeding the shoulder of the street. The voter was frustrated that city hall had not yet addressed the fallen tree. The candidate took note of it and later inquired with city hall. That kind of interest and care makes voters feel you would be just as accessible and helpful in office. By the way, that tree was cleaned up by the town—talk about getting something done before serving in office!

Once you have a universe identified, you are going to start to canvass to reach voters. As you look at the first person on your list, know that *this* voter is critical to your election. With each conversation, you're one vote closer to that WIN number. People will live together in that household, too, and suddenly, one conversation could multiply to two, three, or four voters.

Take a step back to give the voter space as they answer their door. Then, be prepared for anything with the goal of pitching your candidacy and asking for their vote. I have been invited into people's homes (and politely declined because I wanted to keep moving) and one time was told, "My wife wanted to meet you! Come around back." Walking around the house through the yard I was thinking, *What . . . is . . . happening?* Sure enough, his wife was having a summer get-together with friends, and they were discussing my candidacy. They were shocked I was knocking on their door as they were talking about me, and I was just as surprised to hear people actually talking about *my* candidacy. Door knocking can give you a morale boost, as this did to me, and motivate you to keep going. Many people *are* thinking about who to vote for, and you need to go and meet them.

READY TO DOOR KNOCK

You know your district best, whether you are running up the stairs of an apartment building or down country roads. You also will have a sense of timing, as you should not door knock at the crack of dawn on a weekend, nor should you door knock once the sun sets.

Set yourself up for success by making sure you have everything you need in your car (or bag) before you go door knocking:

DOOR KNOCKING CHECKLIST

- ☐ Check your appearance— are you put together?
- ☐ Comfortable sneakers
- ☐ Bottle of water
- ☐ A fully charged phone
- ☐ Canvassing list with clipboard
- ☐ Palm cards, plus ones that have "Sorry I missed you!" handwritten on them
- ☐ Voter registration forms (or the website if you can register online)
- ☐ Dog bones
- ☐ Umbrella
- ☐ Snack (protein bar, nuts, fruit)

You will have a walking list, which is a list of the voters you will be contacting, either printed on paper or electronically on your phone, which voter list vendors provide. Even if you lose cell service, it will sync your data the next time your phone connects to the internet.

Appearance is important when you are before voters. You don't need to dress in business casual attire when door knocking (especially on hot days), but you should look presentable in a way that fits your district, whether it's a rural farmland or inner-city area. *Fashion stops at the ankle, though—always wear comfortable shoes!* So people can clearly identify you, wear a nametag or a button, the quintessential symbol of a political campaign in America.

Often, candidates will walk with a partner if they are covering a neighborhood, or share their location on their phone with a trusted team member with safety in mind. That's because you never know what might happen while door knocking. It was another summer day when I was knocking on a door on behalf of a candidate with a local councilman, and we noticed the bushes by the door were smoking. *Smoking?* As we knocked and rang the doorbell with urgency, the homeowner came around from her pool, and at this point, we were yelling, "You have a fire!" Apparently, her husband removed weeds by lighting them on fire on this hot day. The underground roots were smoldering and lit the bushes above ablaze as we were standing there. After we dealt with the bushes and helped hose them down, we pivoted—somehow—to letting her know we were door knocking for a local candidate. Needless to say, we earned her vote.

PALM CARD

A palm card (or leaflet) is a sturdy piece of paper with your logo, photo, and date of the election with early voting information. The palm card should not have too much text but evoke some kind of emotion while communicating what you plan to do. You should share why you are running and what your priorities will be in office. Noting your social media channels, phone number, and website will help if voters want to look further into your candidacy.

VOTE FOR ME

Your inner monologue will be rolling as you door knock.

> *Knock-knock.*
> *Deep breath.*
> *The light is on, they must be home.*
> *Oh, nice paint color.*
> *I think someone is coming to the door.*
> *Maybe not, it's been a minute now . . .*
> "Oh, hi there! How are you today?"

As you approach the door, look for indicators of what this voter may care about. Do they have any lawn signs, bumper stickers, or evidence of priorities? If they have your state university on bumper stickers, chances are they have kids attending school there. Is the driveway full of antique cars, potted garden vegetables, or toys on the deck? You can learn something about them which can aid in conversation.

If they answer, you'll identify yourself in a friendly manner, say what you are running for, and ask what's on their mind. Never ask the voter if they have a minute to talk. No one *really* has the time; we make the time. So, asking for their time makes the voter feel *this is going to be a real time commitment*. Once they answer their door, get right to it by introducing yourself. Some voters may have thoughts, and others won't but may listen to you. Follow their lead, and ultimately pitch your candidacy. Then, hand them your palm card, and with that they may offer something for you to work with, for example, "You know, what is going on with the schools? Why are they so underfunded? It's outrageous!" Now you have some information: They believe the schools are underfunded, and they are not happy about it. Always look for a way to find common ground with the voter, and listen to their opinions with respect.

Other voters will not give you a sense of where they stand, and in those instances, you still want to make your pitch and leave them with information. Alternatively, others may keep chatting for a while, and you will need to conclude the conversation to meet other neighbors. While a longer conversation can be delightful (or the opposite—someone grilling you on every topic), you need to manage your time. Depending on the time you have available, you may even go back and knock on these doors again, particularly for people who did not commit to voting for you yet, which we will discuss.

MOTION DETECTED

Increasingly, candidates are staring at a home security camera knowing full well the resident is watching from afar, or even from a corner of their home, unwilling to answer the door. I have door knocked with many candidates who will leave a message on the voter's motion device, as if it were a thirty-second infomercial live on their doorstep. You can say who you are and that you are in the neighborhood to introduce yourself. Sometimes, the homeowner will start to talk to you virtually, as you stand on their doorstep talking to them about your race. Voter contact (even through a security camera) is still voter contact.

IDENTIFYING THE VOTER

At the conclusion of each conversation, you will ask the voter if you can count on their support. Pause and allow them to answer. Thank them for their time no matter their answer, move along, and as you are walking away, identify (ID) how the conversation went in your database. Having a volunteer with you helps, and with the power of technology, you can input it into your voter database and move to the next house. IDing a voter in politics is universal through a scale of one to five:

1. Committed to supporting you
2. Leaning toward supporting you

3. Not committed
4. Leaning toward your opponent
5. Committed to your opponent

Many voters will not tell you *exactly* where they stand in the race. They may not be tuned into the race yet, don't know enough about you, or simply want to keep their preference private. Use your judgment as to how the conversation went, and err on the side of noncommitted when in doubt. If someone had a nice conversation with you but clearly said they are not sure yet, do not mark them as a 1 (supporting you). Be honest with yourself and your campaign, as this information will be helpful later.

Having meaningful conversations while door knocking is good practice in keeping you on your toes about community matters and speaking about the same issue in different ways. You may be surprised by the issues that are on voters' minds. Is there a campaign issue you had not identified that you are now being asked about? Is there an issue bubbling up that you can get ahead of in your messaging?

When you have a great conversation, consider writing that person a handwritten note afterward to strengthen the relationship. It won't be forgotten by that voter. As you door knock, you will go from trepidation to a laser focus as to how many doors you can get to in a day because you will see the tangible difference it can make. People will share with family or friends that you have been on their street or were in their apartment building. In fact, when I was door knocking in one of my local races, a woman opened the door *before* I could even knock and said, "Jimmy Tickey." *Wow*, I thought. "Yes, that's me!" I responded. Unbeknownst to me, I had knocked on her daughter's door in town the day before, and today, here I am in another part of town. We are human beings that enjoy connection, and we talk with others about it, so a canvassing effort can have a multiplier effect as you are making connections across the district.

Have treats handy in case dogs start barking or come to the door with the owner (always ask the voter if you may give a dog treat). Usually, when you hear a dog come to the window at your first knock, the voter is likely not home, and they are protecting their house. If you hear dogs bark and go farther into their house, the dogs are telling their family someone is here.

Of course, not every door you knock on will be answered. In those instances, leave your palm card with a handwritten note saying, "Sorry I missed you!" Write these out *beforehand* and keep them separate so when a voter is not home, you can quickly drop off that handwritten palm card. Always leave this on their door handle or in the door jamb, never in or on one's United States Postal Service mailbox. You will then mark that voter as "Not Home," so the campaign has a record of an attempt but no voter contact. Don't get demoralized when people are not there to answer the door; just keep canvassing—your efforts will make a difference.

NOT ONE SIZE FITS ALL

Not every door will be a single-family home on a plot of land, so you need a plan for urban organizing with multi-unit dwellings, apartment buildings, and senior living residences. First, take note of the multi-unit residences and mark them in your voter file. Over time, your campaign should gather all the residences you've identified as multifamily. Once this is done, you can share that for future use, so you won't need to figure out where the multifamily units are every election. Having volunteers who are from these neighborhoods will help with knowledge of the area before you door knock. For apartment buildings, go out with a team and canvass within that building for the candidate. For senior living facilities or condos where you often cannot solicit, ask your team to find someone who has a connection to that location, and talk with the property manager to explain campaigning is not soliciting—it's doing your civic duty—and ask if you can knock on the doors or leave your campaign information at a central place.

If this is not successful, find a supporter living in that development and have them share your campaign information with those living there. Perhaps they will invite you and have some neighbors over. If all else fails, you can mail letters to the addresses in the complex that are in your universe; personalizing the message while informing these voters of the election.

RURAL AREAS

Rural areas will have homes spread over many acres, through farms and sprawling land. Personal contact is even more influential in areas like this, where people are widely dispersed so communicating on their land holds significance. I've door knocked with candidates in rural communities where it's too far from house to house to canvass, so we rode in the backseat as a volunteer drove us. On a hot day, it was nice to pop into an air-conditioned car that was parked at a distance before we went to the next house. I wouldn't suggest having the car bring you *literally* house to house; do some walking yourself. Another time, a candidate in a *very* rural area told me what she would bring with her on a day of canvassing, which includes everything I've shared with you, and one more item: toilet paper. I didn't ask questions, and really respected her unwavering dedication to door knocking.

In rural areas, keep a lookout for trespassing signs and heed caution. In these areas, consider where people congregate—transfer stations, post offices, or local delis. Your town may also have a public calendar of events for more ideas as to where people gather.

While this is not targeted outreach, your options to contact voters may be limited. So, if everyone is going to the transfer station every Saturday morning, then so be it—go and greet folks at the dump. Don't cede any area of a district, even rural areas!

COORDINATED CAMPAIGNS

A coordinated campaign is a blend of federal, county, state, and local candidates in a year when they are all running in the general election. Consistent with your state laws, volunteers go door to door and ask for support for all the candidates on the ballot. Instead of a voter getting a knock at the door for each candidate, they are getting one knock for *everyone* up and down the ballot. It's a true example of campaigns of the same political party working together to get out the vote. Often, it takes preparation to coordinate every campaign's targeted groups, but it can be well worth it as it saves time for the campaigns, candidates, and voters.

COFFEE AND CANVASSING

Once you have mastered how to door knock, your campaign will start putting together canvass kick-offs, where supporters are encouraged to come out at a specific time on a weekend and meet at headquarters, a supporter's home, or even a supportive business. Of course, a nice way to attract people is to offer food, so if it's in the morning, offer coffee and breakfast treats. You may want to have a guest kick it off, perhaps a state-wide official supporting you, or a party leader. Make it fun—an event people will want to be at.

Having an event with a huge crowd and a guest is helpful in capturing action photos. It is also the kind of scene the press will want to cover: a huge crowd there to support *you*! Your campaign will be viewed as having something every candidate wants: momentum. Use that momentum to get these volunteers to go out and door knock. Here's a sample timeline for a successful canvass kick-off event:

SCHEDULE FOR KICK-OFF

9:30am - Setup for volunteers and staff

10:00am - Candidate, special guest and volunteers arrive and guests enjoy coffee

10:15am - Brief program begins:

- ► Host or party leader welcomes all, introduces special guest
- ► Special guest speaks, reminding people we need to work for the candidate
- ► Candidate speaks, introduces campaign staff
- ► Campaign staff moves into action

10:30am - Staff equips everyone with clipboards and turf with instructions

10:45am - Volunteers head out in pairs to canvass their district, and some may stay behind and make calls at headquarters

As fun as the speaking program can be, the purpose of this activity is to *get people to volunteer*, so move people to action swiftly. I have attended hundreds of these events, where I would be ready to go out to door knock but needed to listen to many political speeches.

Try to space out your political guests at canvassing shifts throughout the weekend, rather than having one event with handfuls of speeches.

One time, at a rally where volunteers were supposed to go canvassing, there was a speaking program so lengthy that by the time the event concluded, volunteers were exhausted, and the crowd was lost. It was a good rally, but not the best organizing. A veteran political operative leaned into my ear and said, "Everything has been said, but not everyone has said it." We all love a rousing speech, but by the tenth one, what more is there to say? Let's get out there and campaign already! Whenever you have a crowd of people ready to volunteer, ensure there is a call to action so their presence has a

***

A phrase you will hear in politics is "winning the day," and it is when your campaign feels they maximized the day by outorganizing your opponents.

purpose for the campaign. There's nothing more powerful than volunteers from all walks of life working together toward the same goal. That's when your effort can move from a campaign to a movement.

Just like with phone banking, volunteers can role-play in advance to prepare for real conversations on the doors. For those volunteers using paper walking lists, they will need to drop off results at the end of their canvassing, so the campaign should track what packets are outstanding. As volunteers become experienced, a campaign may transition to a distributed canvassing model. This means instead of a volunteer needing to be trained and then asked to come back with IDs after canvassing, they simply get a link dropped on their phone with the list, and they will get to work, uploading IDs using the link sent. A distributed canvass model means the volunteer needs no training. Before you move to that model, go the more traditional route of vetting and training each volunteer as they gather for a day of door knocking.

Step by step, you'll grow your voter outreach and emphasize door knocking. A phrase you will hear in politics is "winning the day," and it is when your campaign feels they maximized the day by outorganizing your opponents. After a day of door knocking— especially if you end the day with a positive interaction with a voter—you may think, we are winning the day.

For more on voter contact, visit OrganizingtoWin.com

ASKING FOR
Money

★ ★ ★

I know, I know—I can hear you saying how you could *never* ask people for money. That's why fundraising is one of the biggest barriers to people entering this political area. You think you can't ask someone for money, yet you can ask someone for advice, a

★★★

> **Through this entrepreneurial venture of running for office, shift your thinking from asking someone for money to having them invest in this effort.**

favor, even for their vote. The truth is you are starting an enterprise with this campaign, and you need to have funds to make it operate. Fundraising should start on the day you announce your campaign. Through this entrepreneurial venture of running for office, shift your thinking from asking someone for money to having them invest in this effort. A good fundraising program will raise the funds to compete, develop lasting relationships, and provide a well of support you can return to in the future.

In some districts and states, you may find that public financing is available for campaigns. That means there is a system where if you hit certain fundraising benchmarks, there are public funds set aside through a publicly funded grant. Check with your team to understand how this will work if it's available to you and take advantage of public grants for your campaign.

For those fundraising privately, finding donors from the district you wish to represent will help you as fundraising is also a form of voter engagement. That's why I view the crucial component of fundraising as part of the outreach effort, one that will fuel all the other aspects of your campaign. Your donors are your investors, and they want to see their funds go to work.

CREATING A CAMPAIGN THAT PEOPLE WANT TO INVEST IN

Contributors are motivated by different factors; maybe they know the candidate personally, care about electing someone from your political party, or have a vested interest in the outcome of the election. Fundraising is not a transactional one-time event, but a relationship you are building with a donor. When donors see your campaign is active across various mediums—social media, traditional press, emails, and physical engagement in the community—it communicates you are everywhere and working hard to win. Once that relationship is established, you have the opportunity to cultivate it in meaningful ways in the future. Donors are an extension of your campaign, one that has the power to keep fueling those efforts again and again. A candidate who is raising contributions from everyday people can boast grassroots support, and that will lead to a self-sustaining campaign that has people truly invested.

Through a campaign that plays across all channels and by being in the community, you will demonstrate to donors you are building a robust effort. Then, they are more likely to be invested in your vision and feel a part of it—whether that's addressing safer streets, disparities in your community, better schools, environmental protection, or smart economic development.

YOUR LIST AND DONOR RESEARCH

Remember the go-to list you created? Get it ready, because this is the start of your donor list. As you and your campaign meet others who express interest in your campaign, you can add them, so you are always reaching new people.

You should know something about your potential donors before you ask for money—who they are, why they might care about your race, and any involvement they have in your district. Some of this may be second nature if you know them well; other times you will lean on your campaign to do research. It will be helpful to start a conversation with a prospective donor around your shared beliefs. Talk about them and their involvement, and pull what you know about them into conversation. Learn about the work they are involved in and how that intersects with your campaign. We would do this with any other conversation—a work conversation or a chat at a party—so converse in a way that is relational before asking for funds.

MAKING THE ASK

The time has come; you are going to ask someone to invest in your campaign. After the pleasantries, it's your responsibility to get to the purpose of the call—tell them you are running for office. You can talk about benchmarks you are meeting (like a poll showing public support or notable endorsements). If your opponent is outraising you, then say that. You should make the case that you need their support while showing them you have a path to win. Let them ask questions, and without delay, ask them to help with an amount that is significant to them.

You should have determined what that amount is, whether it's $100, $250, $500, or $1,000. Make the fundraising ask, *and pause.* So often, candidates will get nervous and continue to talk, never letting the person respond. You must allow room for a response, and then you'll hear a yes, a polite no, or something in between. If someone suggests the amount is too much or they can't help at this moment, you can note you appreciate anything they can give and will check back in the future. You can also settle on another amount,

Make the fundraising ask, *and pause.* So often, candidates will get nervous and continue to talk, never letting the person respond.

perhaps half of what you asked for, and they may be agreeable to that. Your goal is to raise funds, so try to land on some amount they can help with at this time. When someone agrees, let them know when you need it using the next financial reporting deadline. These deadlines happen regularly in the campaign, and your treasurer will know each one.

I once called a donor who had given annually, and I made a substantial ask that was in line with his previous giving. He could not help at that level, and so I lowered the ask to half the amount, pivoting to inquire if he could help at that reduced level. With a pause, he said, "You are a pushy son of a bitch, but you're good. Send me the info, and I'll get it out today." The contribution was received in short order, and he continues to invest in important efforts to this day.

Still, some may say flat-out no. For those who decline, thank them for their time, and use your judgement to determine whether it was a bad time, or if they truly don't have an interest in supporting you. Take note of that, and your campaign may consider removing them from your list so you don't continue to ask. See, I am not *that* pushy. Some may be evasive in their response, offering a maybe, and you'll need to use your judgement if you want to cut the ask more than in half, or just let it go and keep the call to a broader check-in about your campaign.

You'll often need to leave messages on a voicemail. I don't suggest leaving a fundraising request on a voicemail unless you know the person exceptionally well and have asked before in that same way. Instead, leave a message saying you wanted to discuss your campaign and the best call-back number. Repeated donors are smart and will know why you are calling.

There are some tough conversations that come with fundraising, too. As I've fundraised, I've heard people's views about the enormous amount of money in politics, and they are not wrong—our national campaign finance laws, which allow for anonymous dark money, are broken. I share with them that my running for local office—or helping others running for office—won't single-handedly stop money in politics. We've got to be competitive, and we need to raise the funds to win. Chances are your race is not involved in national dark money super PACs, and you can let them know you are raising money from people like them. I've also heard personal information as to why they cannot give, a health issue or a personal financial matter; in those instances, you should pause sending solicitation messages and consider checking back in the future to see how things are going with the private matter they shared with you. Remember, *fundraising is not about transactions but relationships.*

FOLLOW-UP

As with most things in life, people need a deadline to actually do something, so work with a sense of urgency. With fundraising, letting people know there is a deadline coming up can be incredibly powerful. Instead of thinking, "Oh, I should do that," one will now think, "I need to do this *now*."

Once you have a commitment to give, your campaign should follow up within a few hours with an email confirming their pledge, providing the ways to give, and thanking them for their commitment. Then, have a member of your team follow-up every two weeks or so until the contribution is received, leading up to your next deadline. It's important to follow a process but not haunt someone on their pledge to contribute. Should the prospective donor not respond to staff for multiple weeks, realize that some people like direct access to the candidate, so the candidate may need to call and follow up. Others will disappear and not fulfill their commitment, so always expect some commitments will not materialize.

GRASSROOTS GREEN IS GOLD

While candidates may dream of big checks, don't discount small-dollar and recurring donations. The benefit of these types of donations is that the contributor could give again if motivated. You are also bringing more people into the process by having many small-donor contributions, especially if they live in district. Keep in mind one's contribution is in line with one's capacity to give, so making a meaningful contribution is relative. What is a lot of money? For some, it's $50, and for others, it's $250 or $1,000. Whatever it is, it's meaningful to them, and that's what matters.

As you fundraise, you can show donors what their contribution is securing. For $50, you can print literature for a week's worth of door knocking; for $250, you can buy food for volunteers for the week; and for $1,000, direct digital ads to a targeted group. These kinds of tangible expenses show your supporters the real aspects of a campaign. There's no mystery here; it's money in and money out.

Small-dollar donations also provide good optics for the campaign, as they show everyday people investing in your candidacy. Many campaigns may share the average contribution size from donors to the public. Having a low average donation shows people are giving in small amounts, which signals a connection to people that can't be accomplished if your campaign is only being funded by a few massive checks.

WHEN YOU'RE NOT MEETING GOALS

If you are not meeting your goals, then you need to analyze why. Were your goals too high for a race like yours? Did you estimate expenses incorrectly? Are you soliciting too small a group? You must course-correct, because if you don't fix this, you are going to be faced with cutting budget items.

Let's assume the funds coming in are not where you need them to be. Take stock of the donors. Are people giving in small amounts that actually have a higher propensity to give? Knowing what the maximum contribution per individual is, go back to those people to let them know you appreciate their support and inform them you have a way to go to reach your goal. Ask them to give another contribution, noting the amount remaining that they could give before maxing out. Maxing someone out means they give the maximum amount as allowed by your laws. Not everyone will have the capacity to max out, but if someone gave $75 and you know they have the capacity to give more, you should call them and ask them to level up for the campaign. They can also set a recurring contribution to the campaign, perhaps giving a monthly contribution.

You can assess current donors and take note of who has a good network—teachers, business owners, parents, and club leaders. Call them to give the status of your race, thank them for their help, and let them know you could use a boost to achieve your fundraising goal. Some like to do this by hosting an event or meeting, and others take a less time-intensive approach by raising funds on their own and delivering them to the campaign. Whatever it looks like, apply the same principles and finance laws, and use existing networks to raise funds.

Another shortcoming may be not connecting with *enough* donors. Challenge your team to think of influencers beyond the groups you've already identified. Talk to other candidates who are running for office or have run in the past who may share intelligence about individuals willing to support a campaign like yours. As your campaign has developed, you may have focused on certain issues, and perhaps those issues led you to new people you did not know initially. Let's say you began to champion an environmental issue in the district—think about those who care about that issue and align them with your efforts to raise more funds.

OUTSIDE FUNDING

Outside money may be coming from interest groups and other entities. Be aware that outside funding may be entering the race, for or against you, whether you like it or not. This is called independent expenditures, and they are out of your control. In fact, there can be no coordination between these groups spending money and your campaign. Should a group be supporting you, keep focused on your race as you have no role in that independent expenditure. Should a group not be supporting you, ensure there is no evidence your opponent has coordinated with them, as that's improper. As always, keep your legal team and treasurer close by, and abide by all applicable laws.

THANK YOU, THANK YOU, THANK YOU

Within a week of receiving a contribution, you must thank the donor, no matter how the donation came through (online, by mail, or raised by others). Often, online contributions have an automatic donation page to thank the donor and generate a thank-you email. For those donors who give by check (or cash, if your campaign allows it), you should create a thank-you letter that acknowledges their gift. In that letter, you will include a handwritten note and sign it personally. For those contributions that are given online, you should also write a handwritten note, especially for larger donations.

It's imperative you thank donors. When I raised funds for groups, I would call and thank the donor for their help and let them know *how* those funds went to work; the real difference it made on the ground. Remember, they made an investment in you, and they want to hear how it's put to use.

PLAN AND
Budget

★ ★ ★

Just as you outlined what your WIN number is to secure victory, you will also need to set your budget so you know what this entire effort will cost. You don't need to be a financial expert to realize that every week you will have money flowing into your campaign, and expenditures going out. All expenses and funds raised should be tracked closely to see how you are doing compared to your monthly goals. As with everything in life, you need a plan and a budget.

FINANCE COMMITTEE

Similar to your kitchen cabinet, assemble a group of individuals who want to help with fundraising. Depending on the scale of the campaign, you may have individuals serve on both committees, or combine them entirely. If you choose to have a separate finance committee, it should include your treasurer, deputy treasurer, and others who can help with fundraising, like a volunteer event planner and those with strong interpersonal skills.

Your treasurer needs to be someone you trust as their social security number is often on the line, and if reports are not filed regularly, they are left with a fine for violations. A treasurer's name is on nearly every campaign item, so consider getting someone with credibility in the community. A deputy treasurer is often required, and they would take on the treasurer's duty in the event of an absence. Sometimes, the deputy does the heavy lifting as the treasurer is more ceremonial, given how public the role is. A good team is critical to sound bookkeeping with proper checks, balances, and recordkeeping.

EXPENSES

Raising dollars for your campaign is important, but what's more important is how you are *spending* each dollar, and at what frequency. On campaign filing reports, the interesting data point is not how much money you raised overall, but rather what your cash on hand is. In other words, how much money do you have *right now*? Take inventory of what campaigns similar to yours have spent money on, which will give you a sense of your expenses:

- Social media and digital
- Mailings and postage
- Printed materials
- Technology for your voter database
- Payroll for staff
- Website fees
- Bank fees
- Pens, bumper stickers, or other merch
- Lawn signs or placard signs (often used in rallies)
- Headquarters rent
- Equipment (phones and Internet)
- Consultant fees

If you look closely, the budget could be broken down into two parts: the items focused on voter contact, like materials to door knock and targeted digital media; and items outside of voter contact, like rent, equipment and fees. Your budget should put at least two-thirds of funds raised toward voter contact to ensure you are prioritizing what's most important: connecting with voters. The budget you lay out should be by timeline: what you will spend each month from your announcement to Election Day. Your team should price out each area, so you have a sense of a base budget, and add in options if you have more funding available for a reach budget:

	May	Jun	Jul Aug Sep Oct	Nov	
Base Budget					
• Payroll					Payroll Total
• Digital					Digital Total
• Mailings and Postage					Mailings and Postage Total
• Printed Materials					Printed Materials Total
• Website Fees					Website Total
• Bank Fees					Bank Total
• Lawn or Placard Signs					Lawn or Placard Signs Total
• Headquarters Rent					Headquarters Rent Total
• Technology Systems					Technology Systems Total
• Consultant Fees					Consultant Total
	Total:	Total:		Total:	
Reach Budget					
• Pens, Bumper Stickers, Merch					Merch Total
• Additional Digital Budget					Digital Total
• Additional Mailings and Postage					Mailings and Postage Total
	Total:	Total:		Total:	

MENU OF FUNDRAISING OPTIONS

Raising money to meet your budget can be daunting, but if you follow this process you will have a path to success. First, pull out your go-to list of people, plus anyone else you may have added to that list. Now, let's think through *how* you can bring funds in:

- Events
- Call time

- Digital media
- Direct mail
- One-on-one meetings
- PAC (political action committee) giving

EVENTS

An in-person fundraiser is a tried-and-true campaign activity, but it does not need to be a boring affair! Think of fun and creative ideas that sound like an event you would want to go to. Keeping costs in mind, what's a venue that's interesting? Oftentimes, a person's home is a wonderful location as it's going to be classified as an "in-kind" contribution, meaning you don't need to pay for venue costs. Work with your treasurer so the host completes an in-kind contribution form, which will count toward their maximum contribution.

The host could be a notable person in the community, an expert in a policy area, or even a former elected official. Should you decide to go to a local restaurant, try to keep costs low. You will spend funds on food and beverages, and that's another opportunity to make the event interesting. Drinks and fare from local farms or eateries will differentiate your fundraiser from the usual political event. If you have someone who enjoys hosting or preparing food, they might want to volunteer in this effort.

When thinking of events, it does not always need to take place on a weeknight evening. I personally have hosted many campaign kick-offs on a weekend, where guests enjoyed brunch. By the afternoon, the event was over, and my campaign team would review how we did as we grazed on the remaining brunch and planned for the week ahead. Remember to be creative, make events interesting, and keep costs low so you are actually raising money. You may come across an event that works so well, you've gotten yourself a theme you can replicate again and again. Events at barber shops, local small businesses, ice cream shops, diners, or other themes tailored to your identity can help build your brand with recurring events.

Mindful of safety, on the invitation you may note the event address is provided upon RSVP, so someone needs to respond to receive the location. This way, you are not publishing where your campaign will be, especially since it may be someone's private home. On the invitation, the donation levels can vary; you can have an event that is the same price for all (say $75 per person for a dinner) or use a tiered level of giving that allows something for everyone (say $100, $250, and $500 as a co-host). This allows for people to select a price that works for them, and the larger contributors would be listed as a co-host, which is a naming opportunity on the event for those who help in substantial ways. Invitations should have contact information and any legal attributions.

You will need a team in place to help day of and during the event, from dealing with the host to set-up, and staffing the check-in table. Candidates should never be the ones handling checks, but rather they should be placed in the center of the event, talking with supporters.

CAMPAIGN FUNDRAISER IN SIX WEEKS

- Six weeks out from the event, determine the venue with a host, date, and duration of the event. Establish any themes, confirm speakers, then develop a host committee with a financial goal.
- Five to six weeks out, define the expectations for the host, the host committee, and what the campaign will handle. Set the budget so all are clear and to determine if any in-kind contributions are being used.
- Four to five weeks out, send invitations to a targeted list, and have the committee follow up with attendees. This list

could be people based on geographic location, background, interests, or other data you have access to.

- Three to four weeks out, have the candidate make calls to key invitees, i.e., the largest donor targets or influencers who can bring others in.
- Two weeks out, ensure the event is on track with the goals for fundraising and attendance, and check in with the host of the event.
- In the final week, confirm logistics with the host and offer complimentary or reduced-rate invites. This could be for people who already maxed their donations to your campaign or volunteers, young people, and those who cannot afford the ticket price.
- The day before, confirm who has already donated; this should be most attendees. Confirm the speaking program, and brief both the candidate and the host.
- At the event, secure donations from those who have yet to give.
- The next day, follow up with those who attended but did not contribute (and were not comped). Thank your hosts and secure all paperwork should there be any in-kind donations.

As your campaign is moving forward, you will be planning *multiple events* at once, so set yourself up for success by keeping each on track with clear expectations of those involved.

EVENT IDEAS

A fundraiser's goal is to raise money, and it's an opportunity to gather people and show them who you are as a candidate. Do you love gardening? Have a garden fundraiser. Does your family own a restaurant? Have an event with food from your heritage, and welcome people to hear your family's story. Are you a small business owner? Bring in other local small businesses to highlight the district you are running in. If you can't pinpoint an idea just yet, here are some:

- Cocktail party
- Trivia night
- Golf tournament
- Chili cook-off
- Family BBQ with children's activities
- Happy hour at a new restaurant
- Summer lobster bake
- Weekend brunch
- Women's event with a notable speaker
- Reception with small business owners
- Acoustic set with a local musician
- Dinner and a show at a local theater
- Event at a local art gallery
- Reception at a local farm or plant nursery
- Taste of the town with a sampling from local eateries
- Award dinner honoring a long-serving member or volunteer
- Event associated with notable days like the Kentucky Derby, Valentine's Day, St. Patrick's Day, and Earth Day

Be mindful of summer weekends like Memorial Day and the Fourth of July when people might be on vacation. And remember, the event is a fundraiser—so be sure you are raising funds! I've heard many fundraising ideas and had to decline them because putting the event on would cost a fortune. Be discerning and move forward with events that have low upfront costs with the potential to raise funds.

Keep the venue size in mind as well. If you select a huge venue and have a respectable showing that barely fills the room, the optics won't be good—the room will look empty. This is a lesson I've learned the hard way in early campaigns. Select a venue that will have a space that fills quickly, so the feeling is a full event. You'd rather need to bring in chairs than have a half-empty room. With a good location, dedicated host committee, and a list of prospective attendees, you are on your way to a successful event.

A fundraiser's goal is to raise money, and it's an opportunity to gather people and show them who you are as a candidate.

CALL TIME

One time, I was the call time manager (a thrilling title, I know) on a campaign, and I was literally calling people all day long for funds with the candidate in the same small room; handling follow-up and managing the result of every call. The candidate and I would walk in at 9:00 a.m., coffee in hand, and I would manage the minutes until 5:00 p.m. to raise funds for the campaign. On some days, we would raise tens of thousands of dollars from individuals, and on other days we lived in voicemails, wondering where everyone was. I witnessed call time best practices up close, and I learned a great deal about fundraising.

Call time is also referred to as *dialing for dollars*. These calls can be for the purpose of building for an event, but often they are asking for a contribution without an event. A call time conversation is straightforward: Update the prospective donor on your race, ask for their advice, and then ask for support. This is the most inexpensive effort a campaign has: All you need is the candidate, a phone, and a list of people to call, both current and prospective donors.

Remember, a prospective donor is someone who hasn't given to you yet. You can even have a staff person join you to double-dial, where both are calling out to targeted donors, and as you get a live person, you transfer it to the candidate.

You need a list to call from—a combination of supporters and prospects your team identified. This is yet another reason why your team should always be identifying new people and bringing them into the process. Take notes about the call, from personal information that would help as you grow the relationship (think of kids' names and hobbies) and what level of contribution they committed to. Then, immediately move onto your next call. Keep making calls for a set amount of time; even sixty minutes can yield contacts and funds. Follow-up emails can be sent after the conversations so that donors have the necessary information to make the donation. You can also text the donor the website link if they prefer.

TEXTING

Increasingly, people much prefer texting over talking on the phone, so experiment with texting as a fundraising tool and see how it does. For example, send a text after announcing your candidacy:

> Hi, this is *(candidate name)*, I just announced my candidacy for the City Council. This will be a tough race, but I am determined to win to deliver for working people in our city. A lot of people are watching this campaign launch, and your contribution will help me start our campaign strong. Please donate here.

You can send these out personally or invest in a texting program for mass text messaging. Find the moments in the campaign where a fundraising text is most appropriate, and have it serve a purpose with a time-sensitive appeal, like before a debate, or by a finance reporting deadline.

EMAIL

Our inboxes are overflowing, yet email is still a component of how you get your message out. Realize that a campaign is a series of moments, so what important things are you going to say over the course of the campaign? Well, you will announce your candidacy,

Move away from fundraising gimmicks and ask for real amounts, explaining how this will help you.

release a list of policy positions, get the party endorsement, comment on news relevant to your campaign, ask supporters to tune into debates, and release endorsements. Importantly, you will ask your list to volunteer and contribute. I suggest forming a calendar where your campaign will schedule emails, so you have a plan.

Find the right cadence of email sending—not writing people an email every day but with some regularity. I always caution candidates to avoid gimmick fundraising tactics that some national groups use. No, the sky will not fall if people don't donate $3 to your local council race. Move away from fundraising gimmicks and ask for real amounts, explaining how this will help you. Don't wait until the end of the email to make the ask either; get to the ask up front and repeat it again later.

Find a contact management system that will manage your contacts, many of which are free or inexpensive. These systems will allow you to have a file on every person with their email address, and it will report information like what emails they open. There are also vendors that will integrate the email system with your own campaign database.

MAIL SOLICITATION

Direct mail solicitations have decreased with the rise of texting and email, but they are still an option in your toolkit. A solicitation is a long-form printed letter, often two pages, where you lay out your candidacy, what's at stake in the election and your priorities, and ask people to help with a contribution before a deadline. The letter will be accompanied with an envelope so a check can be sent back to the campaign. While some may send a check in the mail, most will go online and give through your website. Solicitation letters have value in providing another communication touchpoint, explaining the work you are doing and how the campaign is going. If the number of letters is not overwhelming, the candidate can sign their name and write a quick note. Candidates can do this during car time or other downtime, which we will discuss.

ONE-ON-ONE MEETINGS

A personal touch to fundraising increases the response rate significantly, so consider in-person meetings. You can do this by asking someone who is capable of helping in a substantial way for a coffee or lunch. When you do, talk to them about your candidacy and what fundraising benchmarks you need to meet to be competitive. Keep in mind some people value efficiency, so they may prefer a virtual meeting as opposed to an in-person meeting, and they will be honest with you about that. Be sure to research the person so you know something about them before having a conversation and asking for a contribution.

PAC GIVING

One area you may want to look into is Political Action Committee (PAC) giving. Following your local and state rules, a PAC is a political arm of a group. It may be either state-based or a federal PAC. For example, every union organization has a PAC, and they may be inclined to help you if you are a union candidate, or running on a platform for working people. These PAC contributions still have a maximum contribution, as individuals do, so do your research and see if there's a PAC in your area that supports candidates like you. There are PACs supporting fellow women candidates, science-believing candidates, LGBTQ+ candidates, and so on. These contributions often come with a candidate questionnaire, which you will need to complete in order to be considered for a PAC contribution. We will talk more about questionnaires later.

FINANCE PLAN

A candidate should be spending their time raising funds and talking to voters. Working with your team, lay out a finance timeline of how these methods can be leveraged to help you achieve your fundraising

The sooner you get to your financial goal, the sooner you can spend the rest of the campaign talking to voters.

goals, which you previously developed. The sooner you get to your financial goal, the sooner you can spend the rest of the campaign talking to voters. Taking these tactics together, you now want to create a finance plan divided by month:

MAY

Event - Kick-off Fundraiser

Texting

Call Time

Solicitation Letter

Email Program

TOTAL FUNDRAISING GOAL

JUNE

Event - Summer BBQ Fundraiser

Texting

Call Time

1:1 Meetings

Email Program

TOTAL FUNDRAISING GOAL

JULY

Event - Cocktail Party

Call Time

Solicitation Letter

Email Program

TOTAL FUNDRAISING GOAL

AUGUST

Event - Garden Party at Supporter's Home

Call Time

Solicitation Letter

Email Program

TOTAL FUNDRAISING GOAL

SEPTEMBER

Event - Women's Brunch with Speaker

Event - Young Professionals Reception

Event - High-Dollar Fundraiser

1:1 Meetings

Call Time

Texting

Email Program

TOTAL FUNDRAISING GOAL

OCTOBER

Event - Low-Dollar Fundraiser

Call Time

Texting

Email Program

TOTAL FUNDRAISING GOAL

NOVEMBER

Texting

Email Program

TOTAL FUNDRAISING GOAL

For more on political fundraising, visit OrganizingtoWin.com

COMMUNICATIONS 24/7

★ ★ ★

We have heard federal campaign slogans like, "Change We Can Believe In," and "Make America Great Again." Local and state messaging may not be as pithy, but a theme which allows your campaign to bring every issue to one unifying principle will keep you on message. This is called your top-line message. This kind of communication allows you to tell voters what you stand for in a clear and concise way. You will be discussing your candidacy in various ways every day, whether it's seeing someone in the market, knocking on a door, or speaking at a forum, and you should bring these conversations back to your central theme, or top-line message.

While newspapers are decreasing in circulation, the news cycle is still 24 hours a day, 7 days a week and with the help of social media, everyone is plugged in. We are in an environment where there is *never* a slow news day; it's a constant release of content, so your message needs to be strong enough to get picked up by the online algorithm. Even with the loss of local news sources, you will be a part of that public exchange of information and will need to provide voters with content to advance your candidacy—and earn votes. You may even have become an expert in a certain area, and people may think of you when *your* issue comes up.

There's no guarantee that someone will look at all of your mailers, read your entire editorial, or listen to your whole ad, so every nugget of your communications should convey something about you. Over time, a voter will understand your campaign through these layered, repeated messages. When you talk about your candidacy, speak in clean, clear words. Use positive action words like "started," "achieved," or "created" to show what you have done. Be bold in messaging by talking about what you are fighting for, but know the difference between bold and menacing; confidence and arrogance. Voters want someone who will fight for them, not someone who thinks *that* highly of themselves. Confidence will come from a deep understanding of *your Why*; the reason you wanted to run in the first place. You should talk in a way to reach most voters where they are, so use accessible language. Forget the lofty policy jargon that everyday people do not use. This is a communication to a voter—a busy young person, a parent with kids, a working person juggling jobs—so message with that in mind.

There are many ways to communicate to voters, including TV, radio, online advertising, social media, paid phone calls, text messaging, direct mail, billboards, yard signs, podcasts, emerging and niche platforms, and traditional press, whether it's paid or earned. Depending on the scale of your campaign, you may not need to employ all of these options.

Some of the most effective communication tactics include TV ads (cable and streaming), direct mail, and especially online advertising (social media and digital). Take note of what others have used for similar campaigns in your district, and use a variety of methods. For example, local candidates may not leverage TV commercials but will use direct mail and online advertising. Through layered communications, people will start noticing your candidacy, and they may like your next social media post or read your mailer that has been sitting on their kitchen table.

STUMP SPEECH

The term "stump speech" originated from early American customs in which a political candidate would bring a tree stump around with them, get on top of it, and speak to the public. You may not have a stump with you, but no matter the situation, you must be able to shift into your stump speech. Without it, some might think you didn't even mention you were running for office, and they may have *wanted* to hear from you.

What do voters need, and what do they want? Connect that with what you have achieved already, and with the authentic reason you are running. In two minutes, bridge that with why you are the best candidate to deliver for them as you introduce yourself. For example, a quick pitch could be:

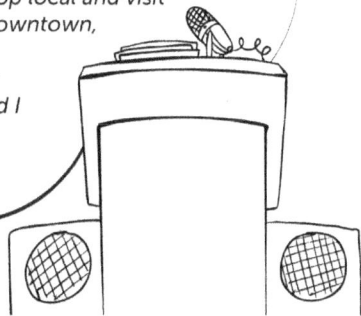

As someone born and raised in this community, I have seen a lot of representation over the years and I believe we need a strong voice to represent the people in our community, and ensure we are taking pride in our downtown. That's why I started the downtown small business crawl to get more people to shop local and visit our downtown. I want to revitalize our downtown, with mixed use developments and more affordable housing options. I will be that strong voice for our neighborhoods, and I am running for Council to represent a community I care deeply about.

With more time, the candidate could expand by giving more examples:

> *I want to take care of the streets in our district and ensure we are paving and maintaining roads and aging infrastructure. I have heard from residents how we must improve quality of life with more sidewalks in our downtown neighborhoods, and by fixing our recreation sites. We can do this by holding taxes as our business district continues to grow.*

When I was running for local office, a friend of mine invited me to a small business networking group. I thought it was a nice gesture, and I was happy to go and meet people in town. Walking in at the 7:30 a.m. meeting, I shook people's hands and introduced myself, and was whisked to the front of the room to address the small business owners. I did not plan to speak and certainly had not had a sip of coffee yet, but I knew a few things right away: These were business owners, and I was running for Planning & Zoning, which is the economic driver in town. I spoke of my candidacy and connected it to a vibrant business community with balanced development. I learned that morning: When running for office, always be ready to speak.

VISUAL ASSETS

We are in a visual age, so be sure to take high-quality photos and vertical videos for your campaign. Think of people who represent diverse constituencies, like students, senior citizens, and business owners. These will be individuals who agree to be photographed, and these assets can be used at any point in the campaign. Set a day to have a photoshoot which will save your campaign time in the future when you are in need of photos. When taking such photos, bring several outfits so you are not wearing the same clothes in every photo of the campaign.

MAILING AND PRINTED MATERIALS

Your campaign materials should have the same color scheme and font, with a uniform logo. As you lay out your communications plan, there are a few basic questions you will want to address:

- Who are you?
- What do you believe in?
- What is at stake in this election?
- Why should someone vote for you?

The first thing you'll do is introduce yourself. Tell people who you are and what your story is before you announce policy positions. Include photos that complement your story, including ones showing you being involved in the community or photos portraying any notable endorsements.

Then, share what you stand for in the weeks before an election. You can do this by laying out policy positions and program ideas. Depending on the scale of your campaign, this can be one mail piece or several showing the ways you'd make a positive difference in your district. Mailers should not have an overwhelming amount of content but should have a balance of visuals, a written message, your slogan, contact information, the election date, and where they vote. A compelling piece will get people talking and may even lead to press coverage.

Ending with Election Day, you'll ask for a person's vote. Keep in mind that Election Day is no longer just one day; it can take place over a period of time given early voting. So, stress the importance of having their voice heard during the voting period, not just on Election Day. Depending on the demographics of your town, consider other languages as well. Here's an example of what a good mail program contains:

1. Introduction of yourself to voters
2. Your priority issue (think of *your Why*)
3. Issue mailer #1 (may be targeted to a segment of the list)
4. Issue mailer #2 (may be targeted to a segment of the list)
5. Issue mailer #3 (may be targeted to a segment of the list)
6. Reintroduction of yourself, recapping your priority issue
7. Contrast against opponent, or a response to your opponent's attack on you
8. Reminder to vote with where and when

EARNED MEDIA

Earned media—or free press—is when you earn a traditional press article without payment often by issuing a press release, which will have news about your campaign. For example, when you announce your candidacy, you'll get coverage simply by entering the race. When you hold a press event, you can send an advisory in advance to alert local publications to the event. A press advisory is similar to a release, but it gives the press what they need to know to cover your event *before* it takes place. Doing good work, and keeping the media informed will lead to greater awareness about your campaign.

Think of ways to involve the local press, like inviting a member of the press to come door knocking with you in a neighborhood your campaign has already covered, so you know there are friendly voters there. This will allow you to bond with the reporter and provide the visual of a candidate meeting voters where they are.

Doing good work, and keeping the media informed will lead to greater awareness about your campaign.

PAID MEDIA

Paid media is advertising for which you will need to budget. This could include robocalls (those automated calls to people with a recording), printed ads, radio, or TV (cable and streaming). For TV, you will need to learn what media market you are in, as some are very costly. For targeted digital media, you'd be wise to get help from a consultant who can help navigate creating good ads and placing them in front of your voters in the right location. For print or radio ads, you can work with local media providers that reach your electorate.

SOCIAL MEDIA

Social media is omnipresent in our lives. We spend more time look-ing at our social media platforms than we talk with some friends. That constant consumption of social media means candidates must figure out how to engage digitally. Your social media should con-vey your personality, presence in the community, and policies you will enact. Essentially, the messaging of your campaign should be supported and amplified by your online presence.

At the onset of your campaign, it's important to determine what social media platforms you will engage with. Don't feel like you need to be on *every* platform, but rather choose a few, and do them well with regular posting. This way, your content is tailored to those platforms and your campaign can manage a few accounts. If you try to be on every platform, it will be cumbersome for your campaign, and you will not give each one the attention it deserves to grow an audience. Consistency in posting to platforms will keep you in front of your voters digitally and give the appearance that you are *everywhere*. Don't make it a goal to be a viral sensation, but rather to have an authentic online presence. If your content finds a home online, it will naturally go viral, which is the point.

Consistency in posting to platforms will keep you in front of your voters digitally and give the appearance that you are *everywhere*.

You could *ask* for engagement, like saying ". . . comment below to let me know what you think." When someone comments positively or with a question, your account should reply, which will show there is interaction, helping with the much-discussed algorithm on social media—noting your page is one that gets good engagement.

Undoubtedly, you will be faced with trolls, those courageous individuals who have a lot to say behind the anonymity of a keyboard. My rule of thumb for campaigns is to not feed the trolls. In other words, do not engage with people who simply are trying to get you to spend time away from what's productive. Sometimes, people will have a genuine concern, and you should address that

Other times, you'll identify repeated comments from the same person who is trying to eat up your time by posting misinformation or mean-spirited comments. If you respond to one, you'll encourage bad behavior because they will expect you to comment every time.

In addition to the communications calendar we discussed, I suggest your team develop a specific social media calendar, working backward from Election Day, noting all the major holidays, mindful of demographics and religions in your district. Then, layer in state and local days of significance. This can include local fairs, sporting events, and notable days in your district. By having a calendar, you can schedule posts in advance, ensuring you are engaging your followers regularly.

DIGITAL ADVERTISING

Organic (or free) social media posts will only take you so far, so you'll want to consider paid digital advertising. This can take a few forms, including boosting social media posts to a targeted audience, paid advertising messages across social media, and advertising on websites. For example, if you have a post and you want more people to see it, you can take steps to authenticate your Meta account for political use and boost that post on related platforms. So, if you have a post on Facebook and Instagram (both under the Meta platform) about your new senior tax abatement program, you can direct that post toward those over the age of sixty-five in your district, further expanding viewership.

Working with a good digital consultant, you can serve messages to segments of your voting universe directly on websites popular in your district, like YouTube. Just as you would send a mailer to certain people in your universe, think of this as serving messages to a portion of your universe online, like to women in the district or voters under the age of forty. The technology is intuitive, so you can target not only your zip codes, but you can further target your own voter list (yes, your voter list to get you to your WIN number!) so the right people are seeing your ad.

One rule of thumb in campaign advertising is that people need to see your message over and over again, so don't invest in digital marketing in the final days of a campaign. Instead, set a budget for paid advertising for several weeks leading up to Election Day. People need to see you multiple times (often called impressions) in order to be effective, and with a budget for digital marketing, you'll be present again and again as people are scrolling.

VIDEO AND EMERGING PLATFORMS

With people busier than ever in a fragmented media environment, short video clips are the currency of the day. Realizing this, find ways to film and post short clips—one minute or less—so people can hear directly from you. The video could be you talking into the camera about an issue, or with a community leader about a topic you each care about. Online users are quick to scroll, so get to the point within the first ten seconds, with good lighting so it's pleasant to watch. Having a good video editor on your team is key to an effective social media presence. Posting regular vertical video clips will create the feeling that people aren't just watching videos, but they are spending time with you; they are a part of a conversation.

In this fractured media space, it's more important than ever to reach voters in niche ways, operating within a communications ecosystem. These sorts of non-traditional media can amount to a large number of voters when you layer your appearances thoughtfully over time. Podcasts, influencer platforms, TikTok, and emerging social media sites, local online shows, and niche online newspapers are all ways to reach voters where you can be a guest on one's show. Ask young people where they get their news, and seek out those influencers in your district and ask to collaborate. Suddenly, people will see you are popping up *everywhere*! This will help differentiate you as a candidate, and we want you to do things in your own way.

GETTING THE MOST OUT OF CONTENT

When it comes to social media, leverage your existing schedule and work smarter. Say you visit a local farm in district and the owners are supportive of your candidacy. You can post about that business on social media. You'll take photos there and can post an unused picture when the farm opens its fall apple picking, for example. When the holiday season approaches, post another unused picture encouraging people to shop local when they purchase holiday treats, perhaps for their pies. You can take a video that your team can splice together to create a series of visits to small businesses in town. Beyond social media, you can talk about the visit while campaigning, connecting it to an issue in town, like local tourism. Since the owners were supportive, you could use a photo with them on a mailer. This *one visit* has now multiplied in content, offering you several ways to gain mileage out of it.

QUESTIONNAIRES, ENDORSEMENTS AND SURROGATES

Your campaign will be asked to complete an endorsement questionnaire by interest groups and organizations. Sometimes, your answers will be kept private, and other times, the questionnaire might be made public and can be used against you given the leanings of the group. Campaigns are increasingly weighing the pros and cons of such questionnaires, and if the endorsement is not worth the time and effort, it will be listed that you did not respond. Mindful of your own politics, the district, and the questions involved, your campaign should decide what groups you'd want to earn the endorsement of, and complete those surveys.

Throughout the campaign, your team should release endorsements to the public. Think of these in two categories: people and organizations. When people endorse you, think of their reach in the community. Those who held the office before you and well-liked leaders may endorse you through a photo and with a short statement, or you can film a brief video being endorsed. For groups whose questionnaire you completed, work that endorsement into your communications plan. For example, if you are endorsed by the local firefighters, you could announce that endorsement during an event with first responders in your district. This way, you have a captured audience who cares about the topic at hand, and it serves as a good visual backdrop for press purposes.

Be mindful of the timing of your endorsements to avoid over-saturating your social media pages all at once. You may want to front-load key elected officials and community leaders so that once announced, they can campaign with you. You may then space out respected groups later in the campaign, or release several at one time in a single press release. Keep in mind how many overall endorsements you release, mindful that voters will decide this election, not endorsers.

Further, your campaign can benefit from trusted surrogates going out on the candidate's behalf with a message. The campaign should think about pairing an event with the best surrogate, someone who has a connection to that very group. Having a credible validator supporting your candidacy can make all the difference in earning respect within a community.

HIGH-STAKES INTERVIEWS

Chances are you have a local paper that will cover your race. Those local reporters will, from time to time, communicate questions, whether in writing or through the more engaged tactic of talking to the candidate live. When speaking to the press, know that despite what the pre-arranged topic is, the journalist can ask *anything*, so be ready to discuss any topic, whether you are given advanced notice or not.

If a topic comes out of nowhere, do your best to answer. Should they ask for information you don't know, inquire when their deadline is, and the campaign can send a response or background information. Background information is data that may be public, but the news source would not cite it back to the campaign itself; so you are basically providing helpful intelligence that assists in making your point to the press. In those longer conversations, know what topics and themes you and your campaign want to address, and always come back to that overarching message. Assuming this is not live TV, you and a reasonable reporter can sort it out and get them information after the fact. Remember, never answer a hypothetical question, which can only bring you down an uncomfortable path of many what-ifs.

Some conversations with the reporter can be set as "off the record," meaning the reporter will use the information for their knowledge but not directly report it. Though they will remember *you* said it, so is it *really* off the record?

BRAND CONSISTENCY

Your campaign is becoming a brand. So, consistency in your message and style is important. Be sure your campaign uses a high-quality logo and there is a synergy of messaging across your platforms. Just as you shop at franchised stores and expect the same branding at each location, you want to ensure voters are experiencing your brand in familiar ways, whether they are chatting with you on their doorstep, receiving a mail piece from you, or coming across an online ad of yours.

So often, we are focusing on who we are talking to, but let's spend a moment on *who we are missing*. When I managed campaigns, I liked to pause at times and have an exercise where we brought together the field and communications teams to find what groups we had *not* communicated with enough among our universe. The field side can explain the voter outreach with data, which may show gaps (for example, we'd spent very little time in a certain ward or district, or we hadn't connected with eighteen- to twenty-five-year-olds). Tie those voter gaps to communications opportunities in an effort to be more intentional around outreach.

★★★

In the spirit of differentiating yourself, pursue the traditional methods and consider all the new ways to reach voters.

The campaigns of yesterday were all printed press, hoping to land above the fold of a newspaper on your front steps. The world of communications has changed drastically and will continue to. In the spirit of differentiating yourself, pursue the traditional methods and consider all the new ways to reach voters. Talk with your team, and younger voters supporting you, to learn about digital platforms showing high usage in your district, which can give you an advantage over your opponent.

PLEASE SAY
a Few Words

★ ★ ★

People mostly fear snakes, heights . . . and public speaking. Yet, in order to run for office, you must be able to speak with confidence. As a local candidate, you are not expected to give one of the soaring speeches that leaders of the free world once delivered. You do, however, need to be authentic and accessible in delivering thoughts without lofty pomp and circumstance. Before you deliver remarks, picture your audience engaged; hanging onto your every word. Visualize that when you finish your remarks, audience members walk up to you as if a magnet were between you and them, and you will be at the center of the crowd meeting people.

So often, the candidate will feel like they are repeating themselves again and again. From emails to phone conversations and speeches, you will share the same stories, and it can boggle your mind. Remember, though, that voters may be hearing you for the first time. And, if a voter has heard you several times, realize that while *you* may feel like a broken record repeating yourself, that repetition is golden from a voter's perspective so your message can break through. Voters are busy, and they need you to pierce through all the noise with your campaign message.

Public speaking tells a story with a beginning, middle, and an end, ultimately asking for action. Good remarks will emphasize what you stand for and remind people who you are; *your Why.* Since you are an authentic candidate running to make things better, you want listeners to conclude that you would be the right person for this position, knowledgeable about the district with a vision for the future, whether you are running for school board, county commissioner, mayor, or state legislature.

If you're still nervous, let's break it down so you can tackle this step by step. First, be yourself by telling a story or using humor to connect with the audience. Next, you need to know the purpose of your remarks. Are you informing the audience? Are you asking for action, like having them contribute or vote for you? Are you telling them about a problem, and how you would fix it? Or, perhaps you are motivating them to care more about local issues. You need to decide this so you can lay out your remarks properly, choosing rhetoric that moves them to action. You can approach groups and ask to address them, and other times organizations will request you come and speak, whether it's a panel, formal speech, or casual talk. Let's prepare for speeches, brief remarks, and those everyday conversations on doorsteps about your candidacy.

KNOW YOUR AUDIENCE

Understand who your audience is, and what they want to hear. There's a big difference between sitting around a table with senior citizens at a senior center and standing at a podium at a chamber of commerce breakfast, so prepare accordingly. Just knowing the audience will allow you to visualize how this event will unfold, and suddenly it's not so scary. For example, if you are speaking at the senior center, and they had a roof leak over the winter, then you may want to discuss support for public buildings so seniors have the confidence to know their senior center will be properly taken care of. If you are talking to transportation advocates, then prepare your plan for transit-oriented developments, with investments in rail, bus, and bike routes to alleviate the congestion of cars on roads.

There are countless topics you could talk about, so ask the group what they *want* to hear in advance. Gardeners working on community beautification may want to hear about your plans for pollinator gardens, a group of small business owners may want to hear about your plans to improve downtown sidewalks to enhance their businesses, and home builder association members will want to hear about your plans for home growth in the area.

PREPARE AN OUTLINE

You'll want to know the format, meaning who speaks before you and after you, and how long you are expected to speak. Are you standing or sitting, and is there a mic? If awards or recognitions are being given, be sure to acknowledge the recipients. Your team can help, and you may even have a member of your kitchen cabinet that is involved in that very group. For example, having a small business owner on your cabinet can help put together your points for the business community. Your remarks should have an overall message; what do you want your audience to know? Break your remarks down in these ways:

- Who are you?
- What are you talking about today?
- Why is this important?
- How will you make it better?
- What is the action?

Be sure you bring facts and figures with you. If you are talking about a project in town, bring notes on the development timeline, budget, and benchmarks so that should you need it, you can pull relevant figures. You do not always need to share *all of these details* in your prepared remarks, but have them ready for the question-and-answer period. It will be more impressive to the audience that you are sharing new information even while answering questions. Be sure to also incorporate personal stories when they connect with a topic. If someone asks you a question you have heard before, cite a person who raised a similar issue, such as "I was in the east side of town last week, and heard the same thing from a family there." This way, you will show the audience you remember voters, and the issues they are facing.

Once you have your remarks drafted, practice using the exact format of the event. For example, if you are expected to be at a podium addressing a group, then practice your talk while standing. Keep in mind a format that is sitting around a table makes for a more conversational experience, where you may welcome interjections from the audience, while a podium event may lend itself to a formal speech. Practicing with your kitchen cabinet allows others to hear the presentation and offer feedback. If practicing alone, consider rehearsing with soft music in the background; this will get you used to speaking with some background noise (which undoubtedly will happen in real life).

MAKE IT PERSONAL

Bring an outline of your remarks, so if you need reassurance, you can look down and be reminded of your points. Hydrate beforehand, then take a deep breath, and remember the people there want to hear from you. Being a little nervous is exciting, but do not be so nervous that it hampers your speech. Connecting with an audience will help cultivate a better experience for everyone, so make eye contact, see what phrases are resonating, and be humorous when appropriate. Never be so rigid that you can't expound on your remarks if your audience is engaged.

When speaking, appeal to both the head and the heart. I say this because in order to persuade—to earn that vote—you need to evoke emotion. Simply providing a rational argument is not enough to move someone to care enough to join you. Similarly, getting teary-eyed over every issue is not going to move an audience. Find your balance of heart and head, rational and caring, in a way that feels right to you. Using personal stories is helpful as it will humanize you to the audience. You can open with a personal story that connects to the subject matter you are speaking about, whether it's an

★★★

When speaking, appeal to both the head and the heart.

entrepreneur speaking to a business group or an immigrant speaking to a local refugee group.

In politics, there are *a lot* of acronyms, those collections of letters that stand for a long title (think FAFSA—Free Application for Federal Student Aid). If you use a local or state acronym, tell the audience what it stands for, otherwise you will sound like you are speaking in robotic terms, and you may lose the audience if you are using terms they do not know.

Always keep your notes after a talk, whether printed or electronic, and file them away. There's a good chance you will speak to a similar group again on this topic, and you can reuse parts of these remarks.

WATCH YOURSELF

You can record yourself giving a speech, which can be helpful not only to hear but also to see how you present. It can be uncomfortable watching yourself at first, but you'll learn the pace at which you spoke, about mannerisms and facial expressions you didn't know you had, and your physicality for future reference.

When speaking, sometimes you may not know what to do with your hands. Don't put them both in your pocket, and don't let them just swing by your sides. Use your arms and hands to make appropriate gestures, and then bring them back to a center resting place, clasped but not stuck together for the entire speech. Your gestures should not be *so* dramatic, but using them in conjunction with your words can actually make your content more memorable. You also should pay attention to your voice inflections and cadence. A brief pause, or a softening of your voice at an important part in your talk can make all the difference in the story you are telling. It's important not to race through your remarks; breathe in between sentences and take a beat in between ideas so the audience can process what you are sharing.

ASK FOR ACTION

Your remarks should introduce yourself and give insight into your priorities, with particular attention to the nature of the group you are addressing. The remarks should conclude by asking for action. You might be asking for a donation, a vote, or for them to support you in some way. If you did not start with a personal story, then ending with one may bring your presentation together with a forward-looking vision. Once you give a few talks about your candidacy, you'll learn how you can add new dimensions to your content based on the audience and gain confidence in your ability to convey thoughts, and ask for action.

GIVE REAL ANSWERS

Never hesitate to pause once you first hear a question so you can think where you want to take the answer. You may have gotten the question many times before, and you know your response, but you'll be asked questions in new ways and may be stumped from time to time. When in doubt, use the tried-and-true acting method of *yes, and*. In other words, agree with a point the questioner made, and then riff off that as you think about how the question connects to your candidacy. There will be times you are asked a specific question you simply don't know the answer to, and that's okay. In those instances, don't make up a response. You may start with your topline messages from your campaign as you process the answer, and then be honest by saying you aren't as familiar with that specific issue and would like to learn more. You can say, "I appreciate that perspective, and I'd like to think about that." I find authentic candidates can admit what they don't know, and voters appreciate their willingness to learn (so long as they don't give a non-answer on every issue).

When answering questions, you may want to be so cautious as to not offend anyone with your stances. In doing that, you may not offend, but you also may not inspire either. Answering a question directly may turn some off, but others will appreciate your stance and offer you a base of support. Being vague all the time can signal a lack of an authentic candidate. You ran on ideas, so run on those ideas! You must trust *your Why*, know your values, and be clear in your positions.

Should you be asked a question that is critical of your record, or antagonistic, don't be defensive. Rather, find strength in your position:

- First, thank them for asking their question and giving you an opportunity to respond.

- Second, address their question, or at least a portion of it, finding common ground.
- Then, bridge to what you want to talk about.

Stay positive in these moments and keep connecting to the audience. If you are standing without a podium, you can physically move, working the room and making eye contact with others as you continue to have a conversation with the audience.

Should someone become disruptive, you can offer to talk with them after, demonstrating to the audience you are willing to talk with those who disagree with you. This may calm the disrupter. But, if it doesn't—perhaps it's a repeat disrupter—it's reasonable to ask them to stop out of respect for others who are there and want to hear the program. We'll talk more about hecklers later. Other times, you will get a question that is not a question at all, but a comment from an audience member. Thank them for their idea, and you can remark on their suggestion, and then move onto other questions.

When public speaking, be ready for anything: impromptu talks, tough questions, disrupters, and supporters who ask you to *please say a few words.*

PART III

MANAGING THE CHAOS

CAMPAIGN
Management

★ ★ ★

I 'll never forget my interview to be Congresswoman Rosa DeLauro's (CT-03) campaign manager. The iconic congresswoman is a fighter for people, never letting up to get the job done. She is the leading Democratic appropriator in Congress (that means she controls the government purse strings) and represents a working-class district encompassing the Naugatuck Valley and Greater New Haven. Meeting at a diner in Hamden, Connecticut, we discussed our approach to campaigning and how every race should be treated like a local election, where the campaign is on the ground meeting voters where they are. She, too, had deep campaign experience managing races and understood the importance of organizing person by person. Later, Rosa offered me a job, an order, and a warning: "Jimmy, you'll be managing the chaos."

That chaos is the art form of leading a campaign daily, and everything that comes with it: managing staff, creating a volunteer and intern program, dealing with surprises, planning ever-changing schedules, working on multiple projects at once, and making it all happen.

CAMPAIGN MANAGER

The title of campaign manager is also a description: campaign manager. This position is the point person for the candidate and is expected to know everything from their schedule, preferences, and pain points. You're there to speak on their behalf and protect them, bolster their candidacy, and advance their message every day. The candidate should be focused on raising money and meeting voters, and nearly everything else will fall to the campaign manager.

Beyond candidate management, you are overseeing an organization—no matter how big or small—of others who are looking

★★★

The candidate should be focused on raising money and meeting voters, and nearly everything else will fall to the campaign manager.

to you for leadership. The campaign manager is trusted to recruit staff and volunteers, manage them, make decisions about the campaign, and implement strategy with the kitchen cabinet. A good campaign manager must know when to be firm on non-negotiable items (knowing what the candidate won't bend on) and when to be flexible (sometimes conceding in areas can advance long-term goals). This can be with team members, external groups, members of the press, and sometimes the candidate themselves. The campaign manager is a strategist, organizer, supervisor, fundraiser, spokesperson, coalition builder, mediator, enforcer, cheerleader, researcher, listener, and vibe-checker. They do not need to use all these traits at one time, but rather have the intuition to use one when it's most needed for the benefit of their team. A campaign manager may delegate the work, but never the responsibility. Ultimately, the campaign manager has one goal: win.

A TEAM THAT TRUSTS

It's important to have a code of conduct the campaign believes in so as you build your team, everyone is clear about what they are signing up for at the onset. Setting expectations and standards around ethical guidelines and processes before people are brought on will help in avoiding issues later. These principles could include transparency in decision-making, and a belief in always being responsive to team members and the public. Arranging your team around core principles will help the team stay focused on what's important. Using the roles of a campaign we've outlined, find the best person for each position as you round out the most senior positions. As time progresses, you will identify people for other roles, first your directors (field, finance, communications), and later key coordinators (phone banks, events).

Once you have key positions in place, cultivate your team by having people understand *how* their work is connected to the whole group. This will allow team members to support one another, cross-train across departments, and lead to better brainstorming for innovative ideas. Before the campaign begins in earnest, carve out a few hours for a retreat for all team members to gather and establish norms. Talk with your team about how they would like to be communicated with. Some people may prefer a phone call and some may live on their email, while others will prefer a text. You may decide as a team to have a group thread or use encrypted messaging applications, so communicate with people in ways they prefer which leads to faster and clearer answers.

When you curate a team that is working, and trusting, together, you will save time and energy. Without trust, there is less information sharing, more duplication of work because some aren't reporting what they are working on, and more energy spent fixing mistakes. Instead, instill in your team—and this means the candidate too—that you trust each other and will communicate regularly. That kind of trust and understanding can lead to productivity. This will be contagious; others will want to lean into the high performance that is surrounding them.

Each team member should recognize we all bring different traits to the team, and together, we are unified in the end goal of our candidate winning. There will be a diversity of backgrounds, ideas, and temperaments, but everyone needs to know each person belongs

***

> **Your campaign team should be working together, using each other's strengths, and moving in a coordinated way for a favorable result.**

and brings their best self to the campaign. A campaign team is like any other team—a sports team gearing up for a big season, startup entrepreneurs entering into a competitive market, or a medical team about to carry out a procedure. Your campaign team should be working together, using each other's strengths, and moving in a coordinated way for a favorable result.

CONSULTANTS

In addition to staff, you will be dealing with consultants, whether it is a contract for data, polling, digital, fundraising, opposition research, TV advertising, or direct-mail firms. These are individuals who are not staff working on your race, but instead specialized vendors who will have several clients at the same time. Consultants can offer you expertise as they have the know-how in their respective areas and can help level up your campaign. Spend time interviewing consultants, weighing the pros and cons of each before moving forward. It is also worth asking yourself, "Do we need this consultant *now*?" Be mindful not to overextend the campaign budget by bringing on many consultants at once, or too early.

Bringing on a consultant means there's another expense, so start small with your core team, and bring them onto your campaign as needed. When you do acquire a consultant, be sure you do your research just as you would with a staff member and understand their record of success. Depending on your strengths and the scale of your campaign, you may not need a consultant for every area. Say, for example, you have a strong fundraising list and have raised funds before in other capacities. Do you need to bring on a paid consultant who is going to tap into your existing fundraising list? Learn to be frugal but not cheap when supplementing consultants to your campaign. Be sure to have contracts with consultants and a clear understanding of their role in your campaign, with compensations defined, and any confidentiality agreements signed.

POLLING AND FOCUS GROUPS

National polling has been off in recent presidential elections for many reasons, including young and transient people not answering such polls, cynics who do not want to participate, and people unwilling to share opinions in a tense political environment. Still, a reputable pollster can provide results as a snapshot in time. Polling can be expensive, but an initial investment can give you a sense of how voters feel, their attitudes, and what issues are top-of-mind through a benchmark poll. Polling can help you understand how voters feel about your district (whether you are moving in the right direction or the wrong direction), and it can give you a sense of voter priorities. Often, you can ask about messages and understand which ones make the biggest impact on a voter. Of course, you can test head-to-head match-ups with you and your opponent, and ask voters how they get their news. If you have the resources, you can poll again which shows trends over time, otherwise known as tracking polls. Do not rely on polls to tell you what exactly to talk about. As an authentic candidate, you should talk about your priority issues and *your Why* that you developed when you decided to run.

Because polling needs to be scaled with a large enough sample (meaning the number of people), one idea you may want to consider for local races is focus groups, where instead of calling out to a large number of people with a survey, groups are gathered in person (or virtually) and are asked questions to dive deeper about local issues, attitudes, and perceived weaknesses and strengths of a candidate in a controlled environment. You will walk away from a focus group with an understanding of what real people in your district said, and that will be representative of larger blocs of voters.

REPORTING AND FEEDBACK

Understanding the organizational structure is helpful in knowing how to report issues and provide feedback. Should an issue arise, volunteers, consultants, and staff should know who their point of contact is within each department. If there's an issue with a volunteer, it should be raised to the staff person within that department, who then addresses it and, if needed, elevates it to the campaign manager. The campaign manager should remedy it fully. If it's a serious issue, then it merits informing the candidate.

In small campaigns, everyone will know the candidate, so you do not need to be overly rigid, but a structure will help so not everyone is running to the candidate for *everything*. There will be friends of the candidate who will try to exert authority, but it's a good idea to ask the candidate early on where they see those friends fitting in—are they a part of the structure, confidants of the candidate, or members of the kitchen cabinet and not in the hierarchy of reporting? Keep the lines of reporting clear so people know what to expect when an internal issue arises.

Campaigns are intense, with one day running into the next. It's important to reflect as you hit certain benchmarks. You may be thinking: *But there's no time!* You must make time to reflect on what's going well and what could be improved in the future. The campaign manager should carry this out personally and bring in others at key moments. Say, for example, after a series of initial fundraisers, you gather the team involved in that effort to hear their feedback. Perhaps things went very smoothly, and that kind of compliment will reinforce the need to continue those practices at future events. Make those elements part of how you go about holding a fundraiser. Other issues will bubble up that you can use for future improvement. One time, during a review of how a fundraiser went with a local candidate, our team acknowledged the candidate struggled to remember *all* the names of the host committee, and a simple fix was to hand that candidate a piece of paper that included all those names just before the candidate addressed the crowd. Another time, the line of attendees was out the door, and we learned that when expecting a big crowd, you can double up on a volunteer at the entry table or add a tablet for virtual check-ins, which moves the line faster. These small improvements will move you to greater efficiency and show your team you are listening to feedback.

You should also ask the candidate how things went from their perspective. Candidates have a unique point of view since they are the ones in the front of the room. In the United States Army, this is referred to as the *after-action report*. It's important to learn what went well and where there were weaknesses, even minor, so you can do better next time. What did you learn, and how will you improve in the future? With your team, maintain what works, and strengthen where needed.

Whether good or bad, you must engage in feedback. Supervisors should offer feedback to those volunteers and staff so you are rewarding excellent work while offering constructive feedback about what could be improved. When giving such an assessment to a volunteer, be mindful that this is someone giving of their time, so we want to lead with gratitude. A volunteer's work may vary in quality, and we do not want to insult them, so take a gentle approach to guide them compared to a more direct conversation you'd have with an employee. With feedback, remember to address it immediately following an incident, with the goal being to improve in the future.

★★★

Chaos is defined as disorder, but a good campaign manager will manage that chaos into organization, where everything has a place, everyone has a role, and every day is maximized with the plans for mobilization, money, and message.

EFFICIENT MEETINGS

This may come as a surprise, but candidates should rarely attend every staff meeting. Instead, they should trust the team in place and know their presence is not needed for the duration of every meeting. Consider having the candidate join the top of a meeting or the end for major issues and comments they want to convey, as well as when approvals are needed. Beyond that, the candidate should be interacting with voters or supporters while the team discusses the tasks at hand. Meetings should not be terribly long; they should represent the mountaintops (the major updates) of what is getting done, not every peak and valley in between. Staff can discuss bottlenecks in workflow, what needs to be done within the next week, and the course of action to accomplish that. You want the senior team to have a full view of the campaign, so use a recurring agenda where each area of the campaign will be discussed, like this:

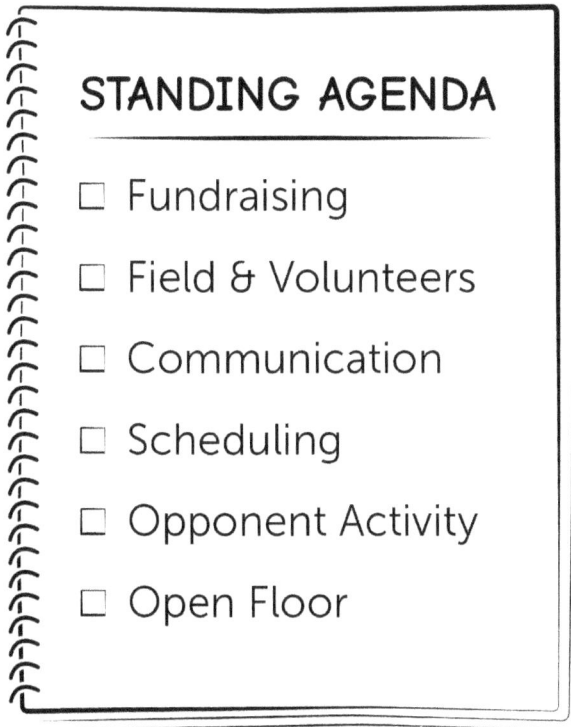

STANDING AGENDA

☐ Fundraising

☐ Field & Volunteers

☐ Communication

☐ Scheduling

☐ Opponent Activity

☐ Open Floor

Should someone want to brainstorm a specific idea that needs a lot of work, consider moving that to a subgroup for discussion, and come back to the next meeting when the idea is more developed. Meetings should reflect a division of labor, with takeaways for all team members.

Chaos is defined as disorder, but a good campaign manager will manage that chaos into organization, where everything has a place, everyone has a role, and every day is maximized with the plans for mobilization, money, and message. No matter the size of your campaign, you will manage the candidate, staff, consultants, and projects throughout the summer, and heading into the campaign season.

WELCOME TO
Headquarters

★ ★ ★

Moving into the fall, secure a headquarters as a gathering place for staff and volunteers, as well as a visible location to gather in your community. Rather than your team working out of their living rooms and cars, your campaign headquarters signals you have an official place in town where anyone can show up, pitch in,

★★★

Your campaign should always be prepared to welcome a volunteer and give them a task at headquarters.

and help. Your campaign should always be prepared to welcome a volunteer and give them a task at headquarters. Having a hub for this kind of activity and connection is helpful with year-round organizing, which we will talk about later.

CENTER OF ACTIVITY

When you picture a campaign headquarters, you might imagine a dark office with papers strewn everywhere, empty coffee cups on the table from who knows when, and pizza boxes on the floor. Ah, the smell of a campaign. I don't know about you, but I need a clean headquarters, no mess, with proper furniture. To achieve this, think of your process—is the campaign data entered at the end of every day, and then those papers shredded? Who is responsible for cleaning up each night? Do you have a key person to handle operations?

Your campaign headquarters is your home, and you have guests—volunteers—coming over every day, so you need an inviting place where people *want* to be. Select a headquarters with good parking and lighting and one that feels safe. You want volunteers to feel comfortable when making calls and spending time organizing. Just a few decorating tips can go a long way: lamps, rugs, plants by the window, a table with coffee fixings, a small fridge so volunteers can store a snack, and a stocked bathroom. I have even seen headquarters with shelves of books, serving as a book-swap opportunity for volunteers. You can also add art from local students to transform a space. Make it a goal to take your headquarters from a messy dungeon to a home away from home where people want to gather.

Your headquarters should have a dedicated, trusted person in control at all times. You may call them an office manager or coordinator, or it may even be the field director overseeing voter outreach. Make a schedule and post it on the wall so volunteers, interns, and visitors see the daily activities, from nightly phone banks to the weekend canvasses. During the day, the candidate may be raising money or meeting people in the community in between professional commitments. In the evening, the headquarters should be prepared for volunteers to come in and contact voters. At the end of each day, be sure your office manager cleans and locks up, ready for tomorrow.

VOLUNTEER AND INTERN PROGRAM

If someone were to walk into your headquarters and say, "Put me to work!" what would you do? First, you'd want to get their information by having a clipboard close to the entrance so you can sign them in. You can even have a tablet device with your website volunteer form so they can provide their information, with options for ways they'd like to help, like this:

VOLUNTEER SIGN-UP

Name:

Email:

Phone Number:

Address:

I'm interested in helping:

☐ Host a campaign event

☐ Make phone calls

☐ Canvass door-to-door

☐ Spread the word on social media

☐ Compile data and research

☐ Write postcards or letters

☐ Host a lawn sign

☐ Make a donation

Connecting volunteers with opportunities of interest to them is important so you can match tasks with volunteer preferences.

Volunteers intrinsically want to help, so give them a valuable task that matches their skills. When they finish, thank them and ask, "When would you like to come back?"

From a voter perspective, hearing that the person contacting them is a volunteer makes a difference; this is someone giving their own time to reach voters because they believe in the candidate. Over time, dedicated individuals will show themselves, and you can elevate volunteers to oversee certain areas like postcard writing, phone banking, or preparing packets for canvassing. I call these repeat volunteers super-volunteers. For example, if someone enjoys phone banking multiple nights a week, then ask them to lead the phone banking nights. Grow your volunteers into super-volunteers by having them own, and improve, a part of your campaign. Always treat your volunteers with the utmost respect, and feed them at headquarters to thank them for helping. We could not do this work without them!

Young people may need an internship to count for school credit, so work with them to establish a schedule and develop expectations for a formal internship. I would develop an intern program on campaigns I managed, and it was a win-win: We had someone working regularly for us in various campaign departments, and they secured credit as a part of their school requirements. Many interns who worked with me went on to serve as campaign managers, and run for office, too.

Be creative with volunteer opportunities, thinking through ideas with your team for new approaches, especially if they come with little to no financial cost. What are new ways to recruit volunteers? What tasks around the headquarters could we use help with? What VIP (very important person) could we bring into headquarters that might be a draw to attract volunteers? These are the ideas the team should think of to keep the operations fresh and fun.

As a campaign manager to a major race, you will not only be aiding that one campaign, but interacting with other same-party candidates. Many will call it a ticket, or a team, of candidates who are running for different offices from the same party because they share a line on the ballot. When I was managing that congressional campaign in my early twenties, I would pop into headquarters across the district and thank volunteers who were making phone calls for the candidates, and other times I met teams of volunteers in neighborhoods to kick-off a canvass and knock on doors myself. Spending time in the field with the people who are carrying out this work is beneficial as you will see and hear what's happening on the ground for yourself. By staying tuned in, you'll be more aware of issues, and potential challenges, just as soon as they are forming.

SURPRISES, SETBACKS, *and Spin*

★ ★ ★

For generations, people could disagree on policy, but there was a fundamental agreement to basic facts of the matter. Largely, people (and their political parties) agreed on the problem, but it was a matter of *how we get there to find a solution*. There was a notion that many freedoms for Americans transcended political parties. That's no longer true with an emboldened segment of the population refusing basic facts. With a fractured media environment, people believe whatever they see while scrolling on their phones *must* be true as they are surrounded by an ecosystem of messages that match their already held beliefs; an agreeable algorithm. Your online ecosystem will tell you *just* what you want to hear, so we've come far from an exchange of ideas where people could agree on the facts but *agree to disagree* on the policy approach.

As a candidate, you are speaking to the voters we have outlined—base and persuasion voters. Because we only have so much time in a campaign, you won't be targeting those who will *never* support you, but your candidacy will be discussed by everyone, both in praise and criticism. You need to know your policy positions forward and backward, and learn to talk about them in different ways. When discussing those policies, you'll be tempted to remind voters just how wrong your opponent is, but you need to tell them why you are right; *what are your positive plans for the future?*

Keep in mind, your opponent will be looking for ways to disrupt your campaign too. When an opponent attacks you, it likely means you are effective, and your opposition is getting nervous. In those times, just keep going. You need to be prepared for attacks, surprises, and even your own errors. It's inevitable, so when it happens, focus on mastering what is within your control and mitigate what's beyond your control.

When your campaign is rocked by an external force, you'll want to be in a position of having a well-run campaign with processes, so your campaign can withstand the incident as your operation continues to move forward. If you get distracted, and your day is spent putting out fires or worrying about external issues, rather than advancing your goals, you did not win the day. I want you to achieve your daily goals, outorganize your opponent, and *win the day*. Then, we'll put one good day in front of the next, winning the week, the season, and then the campaign.

GETTING AHEAD OF SURPRISES

I've seen campaigns get rocked by an attack from an opponent, where all hands on deck are called to craft a response, and 100 percent of resources are devoted to answering the charge. Remember that message box you did when you decided to run? That would be the tool to use to get ahead of surprises. You can guarantee that if you have a skeleton in the closet, your opponents will remind voters of it. So, if there is something in your past you are not proud of, make it a part of your story and get ahead of it, so when your opponent tries to weaponize it, you've already shared it with the public.

SURPRISE ATTACK!

At some point in the campaign, you will be attacked. It may be whispers on the streets or a full mail campaign against you. Remember your message box and SWOT analysis, and be ready to respond while also defining your opponent. While many decry negative campaigning, the truth is if your opponent is spreading misinformation, it has the potential to impact your campaign. It's important to assess the severity of the attack. Sometimes, your opponent will throw anything your way, hoping to knock you off track, and it may not be worth your attention. So, you and your team may decide ignoring a frivolous attack is the best response. You don't need to react to everything, so be discerning about what merits a response. Often, being accused of something by your opponent or their allies may take your attention for a few hours but won't push your campaign off the rails indefinitely.

"Don't repeat the charge!" was advice a successful office-holder once told me, and that phrase rings in my ear when someone takes a jab, and the very candidate being charged *repeats* it. If the candidate were to respond, they would only be informing *more* people about the accusation. Even if something has been disproved, people will remember the allegation if you repeat it. Then, you risk others hearing it, and suddenly there is some doubt about your candidacy. *Don't do your opponent's work!*

Should that surprise take hold, and it has the potential to be damaging, review with your team how this is unfolding. Discuss with them if this is truly on voters' minds. In this instance, figure out the best way to respond. Perhaps you can equip volunteers and staff with talking points so they are prepared to discuss the matter. If something does merit a response, remember you have validators—those key community leaders who endorsed you—and they could counter the attack, thereby pushing back without you needing to publicly engage.

If the press and public are asking, you should prepare an appropriate response through a statement. Your response should address that surprise and *move beyond it*. Too often, candidates react and focus on the charge, only making it worse and keeping the attention on the surprise. Don't sit in your setback; address it, manage it away, and move beyond it.

A MISTAKE

Let's acknowledge that 100 percent of people will not agree with you 100 percent of the time. Basically, not everything you do will be loved, and that is okay. But, when you feel a firestorm coming, you need to deal with it. It's possible you made a mistake (yes, *you* may make a mistake). Maybe you did something that got serious blowback, misspoke in a big way, made an error on campaign reports, or something worse (like poor conduct that calls into question your integrity). In those instances, you've got to move into crisis management by analyzing, accepting, apologizing, and moving forward:

- Analyze the situation with your team; do not operate in a silo by yourself. Review the situation and the ramifications of the options you have: staying the course you took, changing something (if it's not too late), reversing course altogether, or vowing to be better in the future.
- Accept full responsibility. When you talk about the matter, own it.

- Apologize if that is needed. By the way, bad behavior should be apologized for.
- And, move forward: How will you act in the future?

When faced with a setback, discuss it with your trusted team, design a path forward, and move beyond it. Take care of it as quickly as possible, and get back to winning the day. You may find yourself having some longer days after that setback; you and your campaign will want to double down on your outreach efforts and see more people than usual. This will show the public you are back on track (even if you, privately, are not feeling that way yet). Sometimes it takes a long day to win the day.

★★★

Sometimes it takes a long day to win the day.

When faced with a setback, the candidate may have been expecting *something* like this would happen, but their loved ones weren't. In this case our family and closest friends take it harder than the candidate does. As the candidate, you will be more concerned how the attack took a toll on loved ones and will reassure them before dealing with your own feelings. In moments like these, you will also be reminded who your true friends are, so take note of that. After your campaign is rocked by an unfortunate event, remember to get back to the daily tasks at hand and ensure your operation is functioning as it was before the setback. Candidates can hold a staff meeting with kitchen cabinet members as a reset coming out of a challenging time. The same can be done for your top supporters so that you are demonstrating you are back on track.

The candidate will continue to be asked hard questions for some time, and your campaign will move forward. This is why it's so important to get ahead of issues when you can. Without doing so, you risk more setbacks happening; a drip-drip-drip of bad news. Repeated drips can create a devastating trend and wash your campaign away.

MONITORING YOUR OPPONENT

You can bet your opponent is watching you, and you should be monitoring them, too. Your campaign should know your opponents:

- Voting history: Have they ever missed voting in an election?
- Employment information: Who do they work for?
- Official voting record: Are they an elected official, and if so, what is their voting record?
- Property records: Where do they live, and what do they own?
- Serious criminal records: Voters may care about this.
- Public business tax filings: This is for anything improper or delinquent.
- Social media: Did they post anything that is hateful?

Keep an eye on their social media and press activity to understand where they are going and what they are talking about. Ask your kitchen cabinet to relay what they hear about your opponent, so you understand their message as the campaign unfolds. You'll learn about activity on the ground that can be helpful because eventually, you will be in public together, and having a sense of what that candidate is talking about will put you at an advantage. By tracking the opponent, you can also study contradictions between what they say and what their public record is. Some campaigns will hire a consulting firm for opposition research, and depending on the scale of your campaign, you may consider hiring professionals to learn about your opponent.

KEEP IT CLASSY?

So, you'd like to make a contrast with your opponent. In other words, go negative. Truth is, as much as people decry negative campaigning, it does work. The principle of negativity bias says that people will remember the negative charges more than the positive attributes about a candidate. People are influenced by contrasts. So, if your opponent has a dangerous view, you could share that with voters on the grounds of the policy. If your opponent conducts themselves in a way that is not deserving of voters' support, then you may consider contrasting that, but keep it to their positions and public conduct. Voters will pay attention to a contrast on the issues or the moral fiber of a person, but leave their family members out of it, and don't make petty gripes.

If you have a contrast, make sure it's correct. Making one that is not accurate will reflect on you. Then, be prepared for your opponent to respond with a contrast of their own. That's why you may want to consider having a third-party source call attention to the matter rather than your own campaign. Should you decide to sling mud, just know you'll get some on you, too. And is that the kind of dirty campaign you want to run?

DEBATE PREP

Preparing for a debate means reviewing policy papers, holding a mock debate, deciding what you'll wear, and everything in between. Your campaign should replicate what the debate format will be and have the candidate stand with a makeshift podium, with someone who is knowledgeable on the campaign issues—like a campaign manager—acting as the opponent. As uncomfortable as it may be for first-time candidates, this kind of practice allows you to visualize the actual debate. Your campaign should practice the rules that are set in advance. If the debate has two-minute answers and sixty-second rebuttals, then practice with that same format. Leave nothing to chance when you know there are strict rules. Your mock debate should include interruptions and aggressive moments from your mock-opponent, just like in the forthcoming actual debate.

Heading into the debate, if you are ahead in the race, then expect to be attacked, where your opponent is going to try to have you make an error so they may gain traction in the race. Sometimes, not losing the debate means you won. If your opponent couldn't successfully have you slip up, then you ended the debate just like you began: ahead in the race. Should the opponent make you respond to charges, be ready with a crisp answer and pivot back to your own message. *As I have heard many times in politics, if you are explaining, you are losing.* This is why it's important to practice with your team beforehand so that when you are faced with a tough question or contrast, you can answer and get back to your own agenda.

When in a debate, be prepared to reintroduce yourself to voters, state your campaign message, outline ideas, and draw distinctions with your opponent. If you feel you are running behind and need to shake up the race, you can make stark contrasts. This is your chance—sometimes the only chance—to frame the choice and contrast your ideas against your opponent. Remember, your opponent does have some strengths (though we don't want to admit it). Be aware of what those are, and don't play to them in a debate, thereby giving your opponent an advantage.

In the digital age, where short statements are most memorable, remember to keep your phrasing without tangents. This way, your campaign may splice a clip that you can use on social media. After all, in a debate, you are talking to the audience, not the moderators or your opponent. This gets more complicated in multi-candidate races, and you may opt to stay positive with your own message if other candidates are attacking one another. *If your opponents are fighting each other, get out of the way.* This will be a part of a larger strategy your campaign will develop in multi-candidate races.

Debate prep also means issue prep! It's a good idea to talk to subject area experts. If you have a supporter who is the retired fire commissioner, or former finance director at the local public schools, you can ask them to talk on background—so you can improve your comfortability on topics—and for them to offer feedback on your messaging. Depending on the scale of your campaign, you may have a briefing book with explanations on issues in your district. Using this briefing book, you may learn of better ways to speak on nuanced topics, be more aware of pitfalls, and note who the experts are on certain topics. I've been involved in campaigns when the candidate engages in issue prep by sitting around a table discussing the issues, flushing out viewpoints, and welcoming challenges in preparation.

Remember that with a debate, your campaign should be working to ensure when you look out at the audience, there are friendly faces. Once the debate is announced, share those details with supporters so they may register, and attend. Trust me, your opponent will be doing the same, and you do not want an aggressive crowd full of your opponents' supporters!

HECKLERS

Hecklers are not people with good intentions who are asking hard questions (we welcome that). Instead, a heckler's mission is to get attention and disrupt, often sent by an opponent. The candidate should stay on message but may need to engage if the heckler has the room's attention. The candidate should answer their question, respond, and remind them that others came to hear the program and to be respectful so the conversation can continue. Assure the heckler that we hear them, and perhaps repeat at a high level what they are trying to address, whether it's about tax fairness policy, or a foreign affairs issue. Sometimes, their complaints may not even be relevant to your campaign, but they are taking this opportunity since there is an audience. After acknowledging them, move on and call on the next question or get back to your remarks.

Should the heckler continue, your campaign needs to have a plan ready to de-escalate situations with a disruptive person.

Staff may de-escalate by offering their contact information and asking them to step out of the room so they can talk about the issue. Remember, the audience will agree with the candidate because they don't want such a disruption. As safety and security continue to be a top priority, your campaign may want to give the local police the courtesy of a heads-up regarding community events.

EVOLVING ON ISSUES

Perhaps you've had a long-held view on something, but as you talk to people outside of your bubble, you have a different perspective of the matter, and you find yourself evolving. There was a time when such change-of-minds was the dreaded "flip-flop," but in showing your thought process, voters will appreciate you being mindful and explaining, after hearing from those impacted, where you stand now. You should not change on *every* issue, but people have grown in their views—including marriage equality, cannabis policy, reproductive healthcare, and other issues—and we should allow space for people to develop and rethink positions.

SPIN

Your opponent might find new and obnoxious ways to get under your skin. It's now your turn to share your side of the story, your *spin*. Spin doesn't mean sharing mistruths, but rather where we are focusing people's attention. One time, an opponent of a candidate was touting how much more money they raised. And while that was true, it was also true that their campaign had few donors in the very district they were running in, where the other candidate had more donors living in the district at smaller, grassroots amounts. Suddenly, the story was reframed: one campaign is people-powered with many small-dollar in-district contributions. Ask your team, how are we framing the story?

CLICKBAIT

Candidates will find there are times when the "press" will inquire, and it's clear they have the story written before you comment. You'll think, *Isn't the press supposed to be unbiased?* This can be difficult, especially for first-time candidates, because you don't want to believe your words could be twisted and presented in a negative light. It's your choice to comment, or to take a pass on giving a comment at all.

***

We have a role to play in shaping public discourse, and your campaign should practice good information sharing, and push back against misinformation and disinformation.

In a fractured media environment, everyone has access to a social media site, rendering even your opponent's political party and others with an axe to grind as a self-appointed journalist. Their post may be clickbait (an article with a salacious headline aiming to get clicks for a nothing-story). It could peddle rumors and lack facts, but nonetheless with fewer press outlets—and an audience for everything—they garner attention. Don't lend clickbait posts credibility. You can form a rapid response social media team of supporters who are tech-savvy to help with accurate stories. This will allow your campaign to amplify positive news through posting, commenting, and sharing. We have a role to play in shaping public discourse, and your campaign should practice good information sharing, and push back against misinformation and disinformation.

CYBERSECURITY

Cybercriminals do not care about seniority in campaigns, so long as just one person is attacked within your network—from a volunteer to the campaign manager—your campaign network could be compromised. When you're establishing your accounts, be sure you are using an email address that is the candidate's or a shared email for the campaign with a unique password—not a staff member's email address. As staff inevitably changes, it can make for a headache down the road to gain access to the account.

When in doubt, elevate anything suspicious to a point person on the campaign for cybersecurity. Cyber threats are happening more frequently, so here are some tips:

- Protect online accounts with strong passwords, two-factor authentication, and refraining from sharing passwords with others who don't absolutely need access.
- All of your passwords should be in one master document that the candidate and campaign manager have, and you may want to encrypt that document, too.
- If computers are shared in your office, be sure to log out of sites every time your work is complete as you do not know who the next person using the computer will be.
- Should you receive a warning about an attempted log-in or see evidence that your account was logged into, change passwords immediately.
- Train staff in the latest cybersecurity best practices, including knowing what to look for with phishing attempts and suspicious emails. Phishing is when a cyberattacker sends an email that *appears* to be from a trusted source, tricking the receiver to offer sensitive data. Often, these messages have an urgency about them, so you act fast without giving it proper thought.

- Have a camera outside of your headquarters and a sign-in sheet inside headquarters so you can track all people coming in and out.
- Store a paper shredder at headquarters in case you need to discard proprietary or sensitive information in a secure way.
- Keep financial information offsite, perhaps at a treasurer's house; or under lock and key if at headquarters.

Are you stressed in thinking about surprises, setbacks, and spin? Don't be! We haven't even discussed your schedule yet.

SCHEDULING 101

★ ★ ★

The most precious resource we have in a campaign is *time*. With each passing day, there is less time to do the work we need to get to that WIN number. Remember, the candidate should focus on two efforts: raising money and talking to voters. There are a lot of demands on our time as we juggle schedules for the candidate,

The most precious resource we have in a campaign is *time*.

campaign manager, and staff. Not to mention, we do have lives beyond this campaign and would like to tend to them occasionally. A schedule will show your priorities, and so it's critical you are making the right decisions as to how you are spending your time, what events you are attending, and the logistics associated with each.

Retail politicking is a phrase used in campaigns meaning the candidate is maximizing their amount of time talking to voters.

Candidates who are personable will be renowned as *excellent retail campaigners*; meaning you can drop them anywhere—from a dairy farm to a high-end cocktail party—and watch them light it up. This style is important, but with the added techniques of social media and digital marketing, candidates are getting in front of audiences in new ways. Even if you are investing in digital media, you must get out there and meet people in person across the district, and for that you'll need to make some scheduling decisions.

YOUR SCHEDULE IS NOT YOUR OWN

You are going to be invited to a lot of events, and you will feel like you need to be at them all! Remember, your goal is to get more votes than your opponent, and to do that, you need to reach your WIN number. How do you get to your WIN number in the most efficient way? By targeting who you speak to. Keeping in mind the candidate also wants a life with family, their own professional responsibilities, and the rare few hours off, you may want to rethink committing to *every* event.

While going to an event may *feel* good, it's not always targeted. Attending a town festival or carnival means you are seeing people who live outside of town, people who are not registered to vote, and people who will never vote for you. Having said that, there is a need to be seen, particularly by the leaders in your district; those organizing these community events. This is even more important in smaller and rural communities where your absence would be noticed if you did not attend.

So, what's the best way to handle events? For major community events, stop into the event, especially during a time when you could not door knock anyway, for example, before 10:30 a.m., during dinner, or in the late evening. If the event allows political campaigns, then have a presence at the event that will continue even after you leave. To do this, your campaign can have a booth or table, or hand out literature, if allowed.

You will also have an acquaintance who invites you to their house for a party, and they'll suggest you would meet a lot of people if you went. While that offer is kind, the previous lessons apply here. You must be discerning in prioritizing door knocking, fundraisers, events that directly benefit your campaign (like a targeted meet and greet), and *then* other events.

Having managed schedules for officials, we often keep these principles in mind. We also needed to differentiate: Is this an event we are planning for; one we are creating like a fundraiser or meet and greet? Or is this a *request* from a group inviting us to an event not created by our campaign? In other words, what do we *need* to do, and what do we *want* to do? We may *need* to do a debate. We may *want* to visit small businesses, but it's possible to move them to another time. And, we should respond to invites from groups asking us to attend their gala or meeting. If our candidate has recently spent time with a group, then we may be more inclined to commit to a different event, with an audience we do not see often. It's tempting to go back to the *same* people time and time again, but you need to be comfortable going to new parts of your universe as a candidate.

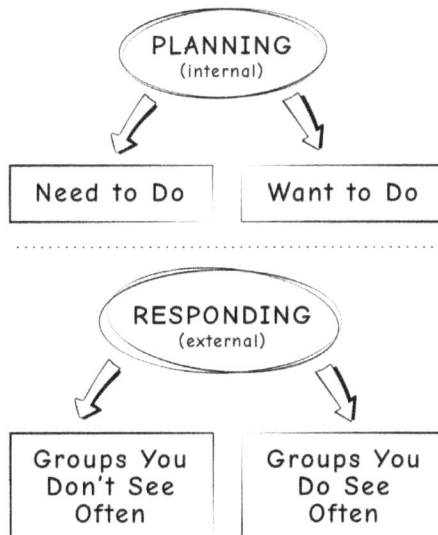

PLANNING
(internal)

| Need to Do | Want to Do |

RESPONDING
(external)

| Groups You Don't See Often | Groups You Do See Often |

IT'S ALL ABOUT THE DETAILS

Get in the habit of referring every invite to *one person* on your campaign who will be known as the scheduler. This person will plan the candidates time, hour to hour and day to day. Schedulers will know everything, as they are charged with getting all the particulars for an event:

- What is the date, time, and length of event?
- What are the location and parking details?
- Is there a speaking program? When does that start?
- What is the speaking order?
- Is there a podium and mic?
- What's the format of the event?
- What do the organizers want you to talk about?
- Is the press invited, and will the event be recorded?
- What happens if there is inclement weather?

The scheduler should gather this information and tell the requester we are reviewing the schedule and will be in touch when we have more clarity. Internally, the team should gather background information using the knowledge you have around your kitchen cabinet:

- Is this event strategic and beneficial?
- Does it provide us an opportunity to reach voters?
- Are there any pitfalls to attending? (i.e., is the group vetted?)
- Does this group already know the candidate?
- Is our opponent attending?

On a regular basis—preferably once or twice a week—the candidate and the scheduler should review the schedule and seek approvals. This will include the events the campaign is planning (fundraisers, canvass kick-offs), and requests the campaign has (supporters inviting you to a backyard party, press interviews). Determinations should be made for the next seven to ten days, realizing some events, like a debate or major fundraiser, will need to be known further in advance.

When events are confirmed, they should go on the candidate's calendar with all relevant information. Of course, once an event is confirmed, the candidate must attend. We want to avoid the candidate deciding last minute to not attend events they've committed to, otherwise known to schedulers as *blowing up the day.*

When events are not confirmed, the scheduler should politely regret. Depending on the nature of the event, the campaign may ask if they could have a presence there, like a booth, a letter that can be read during the program, or a surrogate to attend. This way, the campaign is reflected even if the candidate cannot be there.

TIPS FOR SCHEDULERS

Schedulers are in a tough job, often delivering news people don't want to hear, like a regret to a request, or telling a candidate they *really* should go to an event on a day they wanted off. By being prepared, you'll set yourself up for success:

- Have event background information ready before you propose it to the candidate.
- Understand when the candidate likes time off, perhaps after 8:00 p.m. to go exercising, Saturdays for religious functions, or on Sundays for family time. This should include days they may take off for vacation.
- Use block scheduling, meaning if a candidate is out on one side of the district, plan to do nearby events, or carry out requests in that area, to maximize your time. Batch these

items together so the candidate can cover a few events at once while in the neighborhood.

- Decipher what events are moveable and within your control. Some events may not be firm with an exact date, so find options for those events the candidate would like to go to but could fit better another time. Then, use the block scheduling mentioned above.

- Be patient, as people will follow up with you often since they *really* want the candidate at the event. Let them know you are working on it and will get back to them once there is more clarity on the schedule.

- Remember, the candidate should be meeting new people. Over time, the schedule will start to represent the same groups, so challenge yourself, and the team, to meet new people and travel to new areas of the district to diversify your outreach.

- Keep a list of future events handy; this can include requests or other ideas mentioned to you. For example, someone might tell you it would be great to visit a new eatery in town. You want to be prepared if there is a cancellation and suddenly you are looking for something to do. This way, you can pull from that list of stop-in ideas.

CAR TIME

Candidates will be booked and busy, but they don't realize just how much time they will spend in the car. Going from event to event, you'll be in the car with a staff member or super-volunteer to drive you, and this is an ideal time for political or fundraising phone calls. Along the way, you can review the information you need to know for the day's events—whether it's delivered to you electronically or printed. Schedulers should be mindful that this can be productive time to sign letters, or take internal calls with staff and consultants. Remember: You only have so much time in a campaign, so use it wisely.

AFTER THE EVENT

Undoubtedly, someone will grab your arm while at an event and ask for something, whether it is requesting a phone call, or looking into a matter. This is why it's helpful if a volunteer or staff person is by your side at the event to help take note of those requests. As you are leaving an event, log the action items you said you would do. Whether you write it down on a notepad or keep it on your phone, create some system so you are noting the follow-ups needed, and work with your team to satisfy these requests. You are going to get out the vote next, and you don't need someone who asked for help thinking you were unresponsive.

For more on scheduling, visit **OrganizingtoWin.com**

GET OUT THE
Vote

★ ★ ★

I t's time to Get Out The Vote (GOTV), the final mission of your campaign to bring *your* voters to the polls. Nowadays, you are not building for Election Day, but rather peaking just as early voting begins. Early voting is defined differently in each state, but the goal is to be ready in those final days of the campaign when people start early voting, mail-in voting, submitting overseas military ballots, or sending absentee ballots before Election Day. Depending on your state, you may receive a ballot (or absentee ballot application) by mail, reminding eligible voters that the time to cast a ballot has arrived.

Your local election officials will track who requested an absentee ballot, and who already voted, and that's an opportunity for your campaign to request that information. This way, you are paying attention to those voters who have self-identified as voting early. Your campaign should communicate with those individuals, since you know they are planning to vote using this method. Then, when someone votes through early voting, they will be marked as such by your local election official, and your campaign can stop spending time and funds contacting them. This allows the campaign to continue to focus on others who have yet to vote for maximum efficiency. For those who did not cast a ballot before Election Day, they may vote traditionally in person at their polling place.

People are busy, as you saw firsthand while campaigning. From juggling personal and professional duties, working more than one job, and acting as a caretaker, you've got to make the case to get your voters to the polls. Together, we will cover what you need to know in this effort and look at what GOTV tactics may be best used in your campaign.

DECIDING YOUR GOTV UNIVERSE

Remember those IDs, when you rated a voter 1 to 5 based on their likelihood to support you after a personal conversation? By this point in the late fall, you are going to put those who are not voting for you (the 5s and 4s) to the side and not focus on them. The last thing you want to do in GOTV is mobilize your opponents' voters. From here on out, it's all about your 1s, 2s, and 3s.

1	2	3	4	5
GOTV		FOLLOW-UP		LET THEM BE

If you haven't already, your team should follow up with the 3s (those who were uncommitted) to see if they can move them to supporting you. Have the candidate, or volunteers, make another pass at this group and try to move as many people over to supporting you as 1s and 2s. For this, volunteers could call them, send postcards, text, or even go door to door. As your campaign speaks to them again, change their score as appropriate to a 1 (supporting you),

2 (leaning to supporting you), 4 (leaning away from you), or 5 (not supporting you).

Then, all of those 1s and 2s are your GOTV universe. You are going to ensure *this universe* is going to vote for you. If your 1s and 2s bring you to your WIN number, you are doing extremely well. But often, that won't be the case. If you do not have enough commitments to bring you to your WIN number, then your campaign should determine:

- If the candidate should continue to contact voters as the rest of the campaign moves into GOTV mode. This way, the candidate stays focused on earning votes until Election Day. Many candidates will choose to do this, constantly adding new support while the campaign focuses on the GOTV universe.
- If the campaign wants to include all 3s—those who would not commit to voting for you—into your GOTV universe. Your campaign has spent time talking with them, so you may consider adding them.
- If there are voters who your campaign was never able to reach, but has evidence based on scoring or demographics that they are likely to support you. For example, women of the same political party for a candidate with a strong women's agenda, or voters of a certain age who you focused on throughout the campaign. Make an assessment on what kind of voter profile you'd want to include and add that group of voters into your GOTV universe.
- Be mindful of late-breaking issues in the district and be responsive to these issues. Remember, Election Day is a moment in time, and the dynamics are always changing, so seize the opportunities that may present themselves. If a big issue hits your district in the final week, you cannot ignore it thinking you can just focus on GOTV, rather you must organize on that issue, whether it's a natural disaster, major employer leaving town, or another surprise.

GOTV OPERATION

GOTV is all about your campaign contacting voters in the final days. *During GOTV, your campaign must dominate the field; own the ground.* Just as you did with canvassing throughout the campaign, match volunteers with neighborhoods, mindful of demographics, and other languages spoken to best connect with voters. Some GOTV tactics include:

- Rally – Hold a rally to give everyone a boost in the final days, and tie it with an action; after the rally, get people out to canvass or phone bank.
- Canvass – Door knock this GOTV universe again with a different piece of literature, like a door hanger with your campaign message and where people can vote.
- Phone bank – Have volunteers call voters reminding them to vote and asking if they need a ride to the polls.
- Text messages – Send a text reminding the universe to vote and where their polling precinct is.
- Lit drops – Teams of canvassers go door to door and drop literature off about the candidate without talking to voters; simply leaflet the residence at their door.
- Robocalls – Sent in the final days, these are automated messages reminding people to vote by leaving them a voice message on their phone.
- Social media – Invite followers to share a graphic or change their default photo in support of your candidacy to show public support.
- Group visibility – Volunteers stand outside (often during rush hours) and hold your campaign signs, showing energy for your campaign.
- Emails – Send your final mass email, encouraging your list to vote (and options for voter registration if it's not too late).

- Lawn signs – Get out all final lawn signs. There should be no signs left in your garage or headquarters come Election Day.

★★★

During GOTV, your campaign must dominate the field; own the ground.

RELATIONAL CAMPAIGNING

Your campaign should have volunteers review the GOTV universe and identify anyone they know personally. Then, that campaign volunteer should reach out to those people by sending a postcard or making a direct call. This kind of relational organizing will make a difference for voters who now are being contacted by someone they are familiar with.

Let's say you want to pull just your universe from one local precinct, for example a certain ward you need to get out to vote. You should not mention names or streets, but you can mail those voters what the turnout has been in *that* precinct in the last similar election to show them other people are voting. For example, say "Two out of four voters in your neighborhood voted in the last state election. Will you join your neighbors and vote this year?" This reminds voters that their neighbors *are* casting a ballot and may move them to join in the effort.

A question you can pose to voters to ensure they vote is, *What's your voting plan?* Ask voters when and where they plan to vote, which solidifies in the voters' minds their plan to cast a ballot. It's a social norm of ours that when someone makes a pledge, they usually keep it, and you're creating a bond with that person when they pledge to vote. If someone needs a ride to the polls, coordinate with a volunteer to help get them there.

NOTHING BUT GOTV

GOTV is about being totally focused on ensuring your voters are supporting you. Every moment of your day will be spent bringing your voters to the polls. By the final days of the campaign, fundraising and press operations should roll into a collaborative field effort where *everyone* is pitching in to make calls, canvass, and reach voters. This effort is labor intensive, and that's why you may want to set aside funds for a paid canvass operation in the final days. Your campaign can hire people by the hour to ensure you are talking to every person in your GOTV universe.

No matter how you feel going into GOTV, always run like you are just one vote behind.

Your campaign may have been organizing young people on college campuses, among church goers, or even on tribal land. In those final days, work with your field team and volunteers to have a presence on college campuses for students to vote, work with faith leaders to bring out membership, and be present in every community just as you were during the campaign. From senior centers to transient neighborhoods, apartment buildings in urban centers, and in the most rural parts of your district—ensure each and every person votes.

You and your team have been grinding through this workload to make it all happen. You may have experienced staff turnover during the course of the campaign, or decided to switch strategy midway through based on the political environment you found yourself in.

From endless phone calls, demands from every angle, and wondering if what you are doing is *really* going to work can take its toll emotionally as you are pushing yourself physically to be with voters every day. No matter what transpired in the campaign so far, it all comes down to this: Get every voter inclined to support you to the polls to reach your WIN number.

No matter how you feel going into GOTV, always run like you are just one vote behind. As with your entire campaign, your GOTV plan should convey urgency and warmth; we *want* voters to cast a ballot for you! Tomorrow is Election Day, the most important day to win.

ELECTION
Day

★ ★ ★

The day has arrived: It's the first Tuesday after the first Monday in November. We've come a long way from that first kitchen table conversation and those summer days of door knocking, securing your party nomination, and managing the chaos through the fall. All of your hard work and months of planning have culminated in this moment. As long as you prepare with your team going into Election Day, I encourage you to wake up at the crack of dawn and optimistically move through the day with your team. Parts of the day may feel eerily calm as you are standing at your polling place, and that's because the campaign is practically over, and in the coming hours, this will be history.

VOLUNTEER TIME

On Election Day, your campaign should set up volunteers at each polling place to ensure there is visibility for the candidate. Volunteers can hold signs, and I'd suggest having at least two volunteers at each polling place so they have a partner. Design shifts so all polling places have volunteers holding signs throughout the day.

Other volunteers can be at headquarters continuing to call the GOTV universe, reminding people to vote. Depending on your technology, you will be receiving reports of who voted. These may be available by paper, and volunteers can get the sheets from each polling place and bring them to headquarters. There may also be electronic options in your area. The benefit to this is you are inputting live information and then only calling people who haven't voted yet. You'll make voters happy by not calling them after they have already voted, and not wasting precious time in the final hours.

You can also continue door knocking on Election Day itself, where a team of volunteers or paid canvassers are urging your GOTV universe to vote. Many campaigns will have a number to

★★★

On Election Day, your campaign should set up volunteers at each polling place to ensure there is visibility for the candidate.

call if someone needs a ride to the polls, and a volunteer should be tasked with driving voters to the polls if they need it.

CANDIDATE TIME

While some candidates like to keep focused on door knocking even on Election Day, others will poll stand, meeting voters who are now literally going to vote. It's a captured audience, so greet people as they are going to cast a ballot. You will know your district best and what precincts have higher turnout at various times of the day. If there is a busy morning polling location before people go to work, start the day there. If there is a busy afternoon polling site with seniors, go at that time. Be agile and move around to greet voters. The candidate should always have additional volunteers with them so that a team is present.

Be sure to vote for yourself and advise the press for Election Day coverage. You might run into your opponent. If you do, shake their hand, and wish them well. By the time the sun sets, the candidate can stop at headquarters, thank volunteers who are calling until the last minute, and head home to freshen up before the party.

ELECTION NIGHT

Planning the election night party will sneak up on your team. Having a super-volunteer handle this or a family member can help as the campaign is totally focused on reaching out to voters. Choose a fun and easy-to-locate place for your party, whether a restaurant or campaign headquarters. Be sure to invite staff, volunteers, and donors as you watch the results come in. Serve light refreshments and dress the space up with balloons and fresh flowers, keeping the mood optimistic by playing music.

You should have a volunteer at each polling place when the polls close to witness the final run of numbers and the read-out of results. This happens across every polling place, which all candidates, parties, and election workers can witness. Each volunteer should then call into headquarters with the results. Your campaign or political party may also set up an electronic form for people to enter numbers, so the results are populated for every candidate in each polling place. Your campaign will want to watch the numbers for absentee ballots, early voting, and voting by mail. You may need to have volunteers stationed physically at the town hall or local office handling absentee ballots to watch the count and report it to your headquarters. Eventually, all of these numbers will be released, but your campaign (and your opponents) will be on the hunt for numbers right away.

Should there be an issue at a polling place, like if power is lost or ballots are not available for a portion of the day, your campaign should work with your legal team and political party for a court injunction to keep that polling place open so as to not disenfranchise any votes. It seems like every election, a campaign is impacted by something out of their control, and a court will order a remedy, often having the polling place remain open for an extra hour so everyone has the right to exercise their vote.

The period of time from when polls close to when the results are known will feel like forever. Yet, soon enough your team will see the writing on the wall. Did you outperform in places you thought would be difficult? Did you lose in your own neighborhood? It will be an emotional rollercoaster, but you and your team will see these numbers as they are reported. Soon, you'll know the result and word will spread, so be prepared to address your crowd.

THE RESULTS ARE IN

The campaign should have a sense of what they will say based on various results, so when the result comes in, be ready:

- A too-close-to-call campaign – Often, the candidates will talk about monitoring every vote, and if it falls within the margin of a recount, you'll need lawyers ready. Recounts are different in every state, so know the law in your jurisdiction for what constitutes a mandatory recount and prepare with your legal team. A truly too-close-to-call election will usually see candidates noting this was a tough campaign and every vote mattered, and it looks like it's going to come down to just a few votes, and we will know more soon.
- A loss – Sometimes, despite your best effort, there can be atmospherics you cannot control, like enthusiasm (for or

against you), timing, partisanship too strong to overcome, poor top-of-ballot performance that is a drag on the ticket, or a surprise you were out-maneuvered on. As the candidate, you need to lift others up even when you are down. Thank your team, call and wish the winner well, and be civil in loss. For those who didn't win, it can be gut-wrenching because what you fought so hard for wasn't realized, and it's a blow to you and the team you served with. It's only temporary, though, as candidates often get back to running again and staff helps the same candidate a second time or finds ways to help others. Remember, losing does not mean you didn't advance an issue you cared about; it just means you won't serve in this office at this moment. Reflect on the campaign, but don't look back—we are not moving in that direction.

- A win – You'll thank your team and voters for entrusting you with this position. Running for office becomes a family affair, so be sure to thank your family. You should receive a concession call from your opponent, and you can thank them for running. Celebrate tonight because the work begins tomorrow. Tomorrow, you represent *everyone*. Everything you worked so hard for is now rewarded by a win, and you are meeting the moment.

No matter the result, the campaign should thank staff, volunteers, donors, and all who played a role—no matter how big or small.

No matter the result, the campaign should thank staff, volunteers, donors, and all who played a role—no matter how big or small. After the election, don't forget to remove your lawn signs; a task that friends and volunteers can help with.

Now, rest is needed; unplug your phone and take the time you need to come down from the all-consuming experience of running for office or leading a campaign. A fall hike after the election will allow you to clear your head and gain perspective on the experience you just went through. Spend time with family and friends, and throw yourself back into personal interests and hobbies: reading, cooking, gardening, or even binge-watching shows.

During the month of November, wind down all operations with the campaign manager and treasurer, including filings and closing bank accounts. This way, by the time the holidays come around, you'll have settled everything with the campaign and can take a winter nap. Now that the campaign is over, we are done, right?

We've yet begun to organize.

PART IV

NOW WHAT?

GOVERN IN
Prose

★ ★ ★

C ampaigning and governing are codependent, and while one
needs the other, they are very different efforts. Some people
are excellent at campaigning—building coalitions, connecting with
voters, and showing a vision for the future—but discover governing

★★★

Once sworn in, you now serve *everyone*,
and you are in a position to make life
better for people in your district.

is not easy. Others would make a very able elected official but have
not found their way out of a campaign successfully.

Once sworn in, you now serve *everyone*, and you are in a position
to make life better for people in your district. Remember *your Why*,
the reason you wanted to run? You get to work on that every day! Your
universe is not only the targeted groups from the campaign, but the

entire district—regardless of political affiliation or voter registration. The families of the district are learning who you are, and you are getting to know them. You'll be at the grocery store or grabbing lunch and will be noticed. Suddenly, you are always talking to people as they look to you as a leader in their government, no matter the level. Be mindful that your behaviors and actions are being watched, including what you say on social media, and may be reported on in the press.

Once you take office you should inform constituents what you see as your role—*tell them what you plan to do*. This is an opportunity for you to reinforce what your campaign message was and remind people how you plan to carry out your priorities. A position is what you make of it. You can find opportunities in what the position could be, so make it something unforgettable. You'll meet the moment by keeping in touch with constituents and elevating your work to create something special. Then, people will be coming to *you* because they know you are the one that actually gets things done.

Office holders, not unlike candidates and operatives, need to be mindful of why they entered the arena in the first place; remember *your Why*. Therefore, to achieve *your Why*, you must be clear-eyed in your pursuits, full-hearted in intentions, spirited in making life better for people, and cold-blooded in your path. Now, cold-blooded may seem *a little* strong. What I mean is, this is tough work and there is no magic wand to help you. You will need to make decisions based on data, and face challenges with no easy answer. Being cold-blooded means you are prepared for those data-driven, fact-based decisions for the betterment of your district. As an elected official you are making a determination on a policy or program that will impact people, and you'll find campaigning is full of flowery language; the poetry to the prose of governing.

FIRST 100 DAYS IN OFFICE

The idea of the first hundred days in office was coined by President Franklin D. Roosevelt in 1933, and it was a marker for what one achieves at the onset of their term. Right or wrong, it's become how we gauge success in one's tenure in office.

During a new gubernatorial administration, I joined Lieutenant Governor Susan Bysiewicz as a senior advisor as part of the initial administration at the state capitol in Hartford, Connecticut. I worked closely with the lieutenant governor and saw a tireless public official who focused on establishing relationships between the state and municipalities. During the first hundred days that winter, we visited nearly every mayor or first selectman at a rapid pace—169 towns—to understand their needs and determine how the state could assist with infrastructure upgrades, funding requests, census preparedness, and economic development efforts. As I learned in those first hundred days, it's the time to establish priorities, get to know staff, set the tone with the public, and begin to get things done.

I was in my early thirties and was learning that during these first hundred days, you should pace yourself so you are addressing major issues but not burning yourself out or moving so quickly that you make mistakes. You want the public to *understand* what you are doing, so plan to communicate your actions, giving the public time to process what you are fixing, improving, or making more efficient. Your team should have a priority board with a timeline of what should happen week to week. Of course, you will be met with surprises along the way, but having a plan will help when those surprises occur and can shift projects in the timeline.

STAY GROUNDED

As you establish yourself in office, realize you are doing important work, but don't take yourself *that* seriously. Stay grounded by keeping in touch with friends you had before you ever got involved; and never forget where you came from. Stay rooted in your neighborhood, and remember those who helped you get involved in the first place. No one does this work alone, so stay connected to your networks, and do not become isolated or out of touch by now having this office.

UNDERSTAND YOUR TEAM

You get one chance to form your first team, and your team reflects who you are as an office holder. There may have been campaign staff you brought into your office, or there may be others who were helping on the sidelines who want to work with you officially now. Take a mix of experts in government and people you know well who reflect your district. Most of all, be sure you trust everyone you are bringing into your office. Developing your staff and establishing the

Challenge yourself and your staff to move beyond data that is reporting the problem to actually resolving the issue.

values you will operate under is not unlike the campaign, but this time it's on the record, for public good.

Beyond staff, you will be exposed to a dedicated team of civil servants working in policy, finance, and programmatic efforts in your towns, counties, and state capitols. These skilled civil servants will provide many reports. Analyze the data and gather with your team to brainstorm how you can improve quality of life for people. Challenge yourself and your staff to move beyond data that is reporting the problem to actually resolving the issue.

Focused on solutions, you should have regular meetings with your team and meet with various departments depending on your role in government. Realize that *everything* is important: budget talks, union contract negotiations, pension crises, and the fire of the day. So, stay focused on the priorities you want to achieve while dealing with the day-to-day matters at hand.

LEARN THE PROCEDURES

You must take the time to learn the people and personalities that are around you—from staff to colleagues—as well as the procedures your governmental body operates under. For executive offices, you have the authority to act with your team and legislative body to deliver what you promised. For legislation positions, you are working with colleagues—and the leadership of the body you serve in, like a council president, speaker of the house, or senate president—to advance legislation. Those kinds of relationships are important so your legislation gets taken up in committee, and then for a vote among the full legislative body. In addition to leadership, be sure to understand Robert's Rules of Order, which are the rules bodies follow in meetings. It will take time to learn but knowing the rules your legislative body adheres to will help as you learn procedures to carry out important work for your constituents.

STAY ENGAGED WITH THE PUBLIC

Find ways to engage with the public and put yourself in the center of a room with constituents. The phrase "what have you done for me lately?" comes to mind. What can you do to stay in touch with people and meet people where they are? I've seen elected officials at all levels of government try new ways to engage with the public. While some yield better results than others, all of them show a continued interest in being there for constituents. Try these:

- Meet with groups in one-on-one settings in your office.
- Continue to go to community events.

- Have "office hours" at a cafe or library where people come and meet you.
- Host a community conversation or town hall with the public.
- Visit senior centers to talk about the issues of the day.
- Hold a themed event, like a health or nonprofit fair, with groups who provide services.
- Gather groups in-person or virtually for on-topic discussions, like first responders, public school leadership, faith leaders, immigrant and refugee groups, NAACP chapters, LGBTQ+ leaders, or environmental activists.
- Respond to calls, emails, and letters that your office receives.
- Write handwritten notes to community members doing notable things.

Now that you are an elected official, your presence at an event adds credibility to the organization, and your team will factor that into events you attend, from established clubs to emerging groups. Being visible will make you a better elected official and show the public you are still on the ground in the community. Bring a generic business card with you that simply has your information including office phone number and email; it does not need to have your personal information. When someone catches your ear with a scheduling request or needing help, pass on the card as an extension of yourself.

DON'T FORGET THE PRESS

Continue to build rapport with members of the press and be accessible to them when in office. You may no longer be a candidate, but you now have the power of the office. With that comes attention, wanted or unwanted. With a staff person overseeing your communications, you could give a story in advance to the press in hopes of exclusive coverage about a new program your office will be announcing. Let's say you are holding an event to announce a policy; have a member of your team pitch the story to a reporter. Then, hold an event with a speaking program and follow up with a press release for those media outlets that could not attend.

PREPARE FOR DISASTERS

There are debates about the size of government, but we should all be able to agree that disasters are inevitable, and deserve a response. A water pipe bursting, devastating fire, uncontrollable flooding, hurricanes, bridge failure, or an active shooter are disasters we sadly must plan for. Work with your emergency management team early on to determine how the district would respond to such an emergency. When disaster strikes, communicating to the community with accurate information is key. You can share pertinent updates and direct people to the proper agency with authority on the matter.

There are regular grants for first responders, infrastructure upgrades, environmental remediation, and good economic development from your state and federal governments. Securing competitive funds when your community is in need—or better yet, before they are in need—shows you are working with others on preparedness.

The truth is, constituents may not be following the latest ordinance revision you are working on, but they will know if you came to their street after a hurricane came through. Constituents will need help and have questions, and you can do the public service of providing resources. After the disaster, your presence is even more important as people need help recovering.

MORE PARTNERSHIP, LESS PARTISANSHIP

Being in your government position means you now have an opportunity to engage with groups that may not have been involved in your campaign. For example, if you were not endorsed by the local police union, but you are now in office, why not work with them on a matter that's important to them and good for the district? Forging relationships with groups who were not supportive of your campaign represents good government and will show those groups you are here to serve everyone, not just supporters.

Whether you are leading in an executive position or in a legislative role, remember that compromising on issues is not compromising values. So, find common ground on your convictions and move forward for the good of the district. Find the balance of what's important to you and where you can be flexible so you can make progress on an issue you've prioritized. If you are in an executive position, being a leader is not about pleasing *everyone*, so you need to make decisions you feel are right, emphasizing to the public what good was created through your actions. As we have discussed, people have needs and wants. *And they want what they want.* If they cannot get what they want, then at least they can feel like you listened to their desires.

As an elected official representing everyone, find ways to make progress for the good of the community while forming coalitions. Not every argument is winner-takes-all, so be a convener in office while listening to constituents. If you are in an executive position, you can help improve matters by working with your local boards. In a legislative body, you need the votes from colleagues in order for legislation to pass (and the support from leadership), so work with colleagues to design a policy that puts people first.

Serving in local office for over fifteen years, I worked with others regardless of their political affiliation. That meant I worked collaboratively on a plan to increase our affordable housing stock, supported industry with job creation, and focused on a more vibrant and walkable downtown while holding taxes steady and championing a transparent budget process. In local government, you will see it *all*: We passed regulations on the keeping and raising of chickens, reviewed cannabis sales in town, required developers plant native noninvasive plant species, built roads and sidewalks, approved economic developments for Fortune 500 companies, and redeveloped shuttered factories with mixed-use proposals, always with more work to do.

Not every argument is winner-takes-all, so be a convener in office while listening to constituents.

MASTER CONSTITUENT CASEWORK

I've seen with my own eyes that with your official office, you are in a distinct position of being able to help people in tangible ways. That's why your office should prioritize casework roles, which are defined as staff with certain areas of expertise ready to help constituents. In a local office, you are dealing with local decisions, from the education system to roads, town buildings and facilities, local flooding matters, and your tax rate. In a state office, they are faced with questions about state action (or inaction) from energy to education and state programs, as well as opinions on state legislation. For a federal office, people may be calling for help with a federal matter, from immigration to veteran's benefits, passports and social security issues. The goal of the office should be to work on the people's behalf, finding favorable resolutions for people. This may mean you need to call agencies in your jurisdiction, advocate for constituents, and cut through red tape as you demand action. Often, you may need to redirect constituents who call regarding an issue but to the wrong level of government. For example, a federal office would not be able to help with taking a local tree down, but could refer the constituent to their locality. Similarly, local elected officials are not able to help with passports, but a federal office can. Knowing what each level of government can assist with will help

You have the unique ability to make a difference for someone, no matter if you think the issue is big or small, because if they are asking for help, it's important to them.

elected officials refer constituents to the proper office so government works for people.

As district director for Congressman Jim Himes (CT-04), I learned how to lead a busy congressional office, where no day is the same as the next as I interacted with local, state, and federal officials. Most of all, I learned the importance of constituent casework in our Bridgeport and Stamford, Connecticut, offices. The congressman has become a leader in our national intelligence and is focused on making things better for the district, which has one of the widest disparities in the country, from the wealthiest zip codes to the most economically distressed. So, ensuring when someone calls they immediately get a live person—and a favorable result for their federal issue—is critically important to the congressman, and therefore to our team.

Ensure your office has staff with the spirit and desire to help people. There are so many people who are wondering how to get involved in this space, *and you are the one there.* You have the unique ability to make a difference for someone, no matter if you think the issue is big or small, because if they are asking for help, it's important to them. This means opening a case, and either resolving it by advocating vigorously for the constituent or referring it to an office who can assist. This type of service will be remembered by a constituent. Now that you are in office, you are working on behalf of all constituents and developing your reputation with voters as someone who can get things done. While the office won't succeed with every case, a good casework team that is helping constituents is what so many often refer to as the power of incumbency.

We are *just* scratching the surface to ensure that in your first hundred days you've established yourself as a capable and effective elected official who cares about people and is putting the district on the right track. In office, be mindful of *your Why*, clear-eyed, full-hearted, spirited, and maybe even cold-blooded, for the people you represent. Your best route to re-election is delighting and delivering for constituents every day.

ONCE A STAFFER,
Always a Staffer

★ ★ ★

I've had a unique experience having been immersed in politics through running and serving in local office while working for officials in state and federal government. By day I was working in their office, and by night I was fulfilling my own public service. No matter the role I've held, I'm convinced *anyone* who works in a campaign or government office is called *staff*. Whether it's a volunteer, intern, campaign manager, or a senior employee, the public views us all the same: aides and staff. It's similar to people not knowing what exactly each level of government does—local, county, state, and federal; official office or the campaign side. It's as if anyone who does *anything* with politics works in one large building that has GOVERNMENT written on it, and everyone there is, you guessed it: staff. The nuances may not be realized, but each person plays a critical role—whether they are a budget analyst, immigration caseworker, grant writer, outreach manager, or campaign operative.

Titles are a funny thing in politics, but at the end of the day being a staffer is about making sure the candidate is successful. Having served in local, state, and federal roles, I've learned good staffing comes down to a willingness to learn, a strong work ethic, a sense of adaptability, and a healthy dose of finesse. Events, projects, and tasks will look effortless, no matter the amount of effort it *really* took. This is a bonding experience for staffers, which makes everyone feel we are in this effort together, a part of the beautiful chaotic energy of politics. To anyone who has worked in this space, you'll share stories with each other about the long days, early mornings campaigning, and late nights strategizing, wild situations you found yourselves in (people wouldn't believe us), and the unforgettable personalities (people *really* wouldn't believe us).

With most local and state campaigns being fewer than ten months, and given the sheer volume of people you interact with, by the end of the campaign you are left with more experiences, conversations, laughs, and arguments than a human might be able to process in real time. For all the hard work, sweat, and tears, it's the most rewarding experience to organize a community, a district, or a state and see the benefits of your work. You did not just work for a candidate because of their political party; you believed in them and what they fought for. You've made a mark on the kind of representation we have in our democracy. You helped play a critical role in the campaign and drive your candidate to success. A one-time campaign job becomes a career, and even a lifestyle of public service. Staff represents the elected official, has foresight in understanding how situations will play out, and knows how to get the job done for their district. No one *really* knows what it's like unless you're there, so this is for you, staffer.

ANSWER THE PHONE

I've learned unknown callers to my phone were either the highest-ranking members of our federal government or telemarketers asking if I was interested in car insurance. It was a gamble but being accessible has made for many opportunities. Answer your phone, be responsive, and tend to all the ways people communicate (calls, texts, email, social media) so people realize if they contact you, they will get a response. If a press person contacts you on social media, for example, you should respond, get that to the proper communications person on the campaign, and have them handle it since they are the authority for communications. In that action, you've satisfied a press request, and done a favor for your teammate. We are accessible 24/7, so get used to this reality.

BE A SPONGE

The best way to learn is by throwing yourself at the work and trying to master a little bit of everything. Soon, you will find what areas you are more passionate about and where you might gravitate toward in a campaign. Do you like fundraising, field, communications, event building, or compliance work? By gaining exposure to all these areas and more, you'll be preparing yourself for future roles. Many of these areas will teach you skills that are transferable should you go into other lines of work, such as nonprofit management, business, and education.

The best way to learn is by throwing yourself at the work and trying to master a little bit of everything.

ONE EYE ON TODAY, ONE ON TOMORROW

As a staffer, you are there to support your candidate. Therefore, you need to have one eye on today to ensure all the preparations are done, events and meetings have background, details are set in the calendar, and your candidate is ready for the hours ahead. And, you need to have an eye on what's next; what does the team need to do to ensure you are not scrambling tomorrow morning? This may sound obvious, but in the rush of the campaign, you're going to have last-minute urgencies that will take your eye off planning ahead. Don't fall into that trap; always keep one eye looking forward to what further background is needed without being asked to do so. If you get into this habit, you'll be ready for today while setting yourself up for success tomorrow.

MANAGE YOUR TIME

Keep a calendar, and put every occasion where you need to be somewhere (physically or virtually), or anything that requires thirty minutes or more of your time. This means if you need to set time aside to draft a debate prep memo, place that on your calendar. Then, try your best to stay on task with the calendar, knowing full well that other to-dos will pop up. When you can, delegate or ask for help; but when you are leading something, you will need to maintain responsibility of the project. Prioritize, always doing the hardest thing first (make that call you are dreading first). Be mindful of what you can do when. For example, you can make calls during the day, and work on memos when it's quiet at night.

You may consider keeping a to-do list. Now, there are many days where I am *adding* onto my to-do list faster than I am crossing things off, but keeping a record of what you need to accomplish will take the clutter out of your head and make it real. When writing tasks down, break down larger tasks into smaller ones. For example, you wouldn't say *create event*, but rather you would confirm the location of the event, confirm with the host, and begin drafting the invitation. Use specific tasks to get done so your to-do list is representative of the actual tactics that need to be accomplished, and you may be able to delegate the drafting of the invitation. Be mindful of attaching deadlines to tasks that are time-sensitive. And yes, block out personal time for yourself!

ROUGH AND TUMBLE

Politics is not for the faint of heart. For some, winning that next election is *everything*, and they are playing for keeps. From whisper campaigns to full attacks, you'll experience those who will try to sideline you, intimidate you, or sow trouble around you for their purposes. In those moments, you cannot get scared and retreat. Other times, it may not be as intentional, like on a day you worked hard and instead of thinking of all the good you did, that *one*

★★★

> **Just keep organizing—cutting through the chaos and working around obstacles, even when difficult, with a smile.**

complaint you heard is what reverberates in your mind. Just keep organizing—cutting through the chaos and working around obstacles, even when difficult, with a smile.

SPEAK UP

You'll find yourself sitting around a table with the candidate, where everyone is complimenting the candidate on the matter at hand, and you will be there thinking, *I don't agree*. Agreeing with the candidate can be like dominoes; everyone falls into place quickly. In those times, try being a voice rather than an echo. If you disagree— or have a different vantage point on the topic—speak up and state why constructively. If that's the case, lay that out to the group. Think critically and give your opinion even when it's not popular in the moment. Your candidate will see you are not afraid to speak up.

NO SURPRISES

There will be surprises outside of our control, but there should never be an *internal* surprise. It's critical to be unified and to ensure your team knows information before it goes to the candidate, and certainly the public. You should talk among your team before you make news or pitch your candidate an idea.

Further, your candidate should know of news before a campaign releases it to the public. Plan, communicate, and be candid with your team. You will work better and more efficiently if you have the mantra of *no surprises*. When a decision is made, be respectful of roles and who is best to break news to the public and the candidate.

NO DRAMA

Inevitably, you will have a disagreement with a colleague. In the intensity of a campaign, this can create an awkward day and have a chilling effect on the group. As in life, approach the person in a neutral environment and assume good intentions, always speak with "I" statements (how *you* are feeling), and seek to understand their point of view. Always take feedback seriously, but not personally (there is a difference). Focus on facts—not drama—and respond after hearing the person. Stay calm and find a resolution. Should a resolution not be attainable right away, try not to match their aggression, and know when to walk away for the moment. Still, you are in a working environment and will need to be operational with the person. Remember that while your campaign squabbles, your opponent is scheming, so remedy disagreement quickly.

ONE TEAM

As a staffer, you'll overhear private information about the candidate, both personal and political. Maintain the confidence of your candidate and keep what's private, private. You risk breaking their trust, and undermining the whole team, should you break it. Remember that what happens on the campaign stays among that campaign team. And, even when you do not agree with what was decided upon by the team, you still need to support your candidate. In other words, you need to get on board and operate as one team once a decision is made. The strategy may work or not, but it won't be helpful if you are doubting your candidate publicly.

AMPLIFY OTHERS

Have you ever been in a meeting and mentioned an idea to the group, only for someone to say the *same idea* a few minutes later—then everyone says how wonderful it was? Often, the idea that is praised is said by the loudest voice in the room. We need to lift up newcomers, junior-level staff, and introverts (it's not easy being an introvert in politics). Be the person in the meeting who amplifies others, noting how your teammate had a great idea . . . *tell us about it*.

BUILD A NETWORK

Campaigns come and go, and with a victory, some campaign staff may move over to the official office, leaving others to find work. No matter where you land, you will find the same people involved in campaigns, government, and related fields, so build and maintain a network, treat people well, and keep people's contact information as you continue down your journey. You never know where your future might lead, and who you may work with.

When you meet someone who has excelled in your field and they offer advice to you, listen. Remember, two ears and one mouth! Down the line, offer your own expertise to someone trying to break into your field and mentor them. Not everyone is so kind as to welcome others into this arena, but you'll set the example by bringing people in.

When you meet someone who has excelled in your field and they offer advice to you, listen.

OPEN TO POSSIBILITIES

Once you are in the political arena, realize there are a lot of doors here, so be open to new possibilities. Never be so intensely focused on what you *think* is your next step that you miss other opportunities that may be showing themselves to you. A life of public service means you're open to ways to serve, and they may not always be exactly what you envisioned, in part because you did not know all the opportunities that were available when you first got involved.

CIRCLE OF TRUST?

As President Harry Truman once said, if you want a friend in Washington (as in, politics), get a dog. This is a hard lesson that not every single person you meet in politics is a true friend. Friendship is an emotional bond enduring in trust. Confidants are people you can bounce ideas off of and who help you achieve your goal. Allies are people who have goals themselves with various loyalties and, at times, those will coincide with your goals, making for a fortuitous opportunity. You can have an ally in a legislative fight, perhaps among two people who never work together but had similar goals and collaborated to get it done. None of these exclusively are bad people but thinking everyone is a friend as they sell you out can be most disappointing.

Alternatively, someone you work with over and over again can develop into a wonderful relationship, and that's one of the joys of the work. In fact, at my first Connecticut Democrats Bailey Dinner, the state party's major annual event (where I knew no one in politics), I met a new friend in Sam Carmody as the ballroom was buzzing with speeches and schmoozing. Sam and I would go on to become friends, volunteered together on the campaign trail, and even worked in the same campaigns and offices. Eventually we traded in those professional titles for Mr. and Mr.—we married fifteen years after first meeting. So, while politics can be rough and tumble, it can have some love, too.

YEAR-ROUND
Organizing

★ ★ ★

Yₒu've been on a journey of running for, and winning, public office. The truth is, voters have been on a journey, too. From awareness about the election, to considerations for the candidates, and processing their own beliefs, they made the decision to vote and participate in our democracy.

Whether you like it or not, your re-election campaign starts quickly. Especially when most are elected for only two years, you'll find that once you move through your first hundred days with your staff, suddenly you are looking at your re-election. Aside from your official role, you should talk with your former campaign team and treasurer to prepare filing for re-election. Further, realize that your political party has value, and they can help party-build for the future, so pay attention to your party's hardworking members.

There are candidates who *only* turn up during election season: a face on a mailer, but not in the community doing the work. Should they face a challenge, they will realize the support they thought was wide was also shallow. Meeting people, making connections, and being involved in your community will ensure that your support is deep. This is helpful in case you inevitably take a hard vote or an unpopular stance and have the wherewithal of support to navigate challenges because your community gives you that space.

When it's time for re-election, you will want to tell voters you fulfilled the promises you made. In other words, "I told you I would deliver, and I did." If there were matters you did not complete yet, run the SWOT analysis and message box as you did in your first race and prepare for a serious campaign effort.

As an incumbent, adjust your message to one that emphasizes accomplishments, and be upfront about what's left to do because there is always more to work on. Speak with clarity about work completed and yet to be done. A good re-election campaign uses

Whether you like it or not, your re-election campaign starts quickly.

the lessons from your first, with the added experience of both campaigning and serving in the position. It's not enough to only tout past accomplishments, but rather think in terms of *what's next*.

The idea of year-round organizing has been of interest to me, so much so that I was elected in 2022 as vice chair of the Connecticut Democratic Party on the idea of strengthening our state party, building from the bottom up, and creating more programs to grow the party. We need easy to access entry points into our campaigns and political parties. These entry points are mutually beneficial, so a volunteer may find their way to a campaign, and the campaign's efforts multiply with new people joining. By making our campaigns accessible, we create a more welcoming environment, and continue to reduce the barriers of entry in politics.

Remember when we said the magic of political parties is with its members? It's an honor when voting members—the people—choose you to represent them. In this volunteer position as vice chair, I met members, activists, and candidates in their towns. From Fairfield County to Eastern Connecticut, from the northwest corner to the "quiet corner" of northeastern Connecticut, and from central Connecticut to the shoreline—big cities, towns, and rural communities—I heard what people needed and wanted from their party. From those conversations, I started a training series to teach people how to campaign. Every month, we'd meet virtually, and I would voluntarily teach topics including fundraising, door knocking, digital media, and candidate recruitment.

As party leaders, we are always asking people to raise their hand and run for office but had few resources for them when they decided to enter the arena. The trainings helped with this, and working with our team, we developed more ways to assist local candidates and party-build. Given my background, I worked with candidates up and down the ballot on a coordinated campaign to benefit candidates, from governors to senators; state legislators and local candidates. From a political party perspective, I saw how ongoing engagement with voters can be a powerful approach. Together let's review how you can shift to this kind of organizing.

DON'T TAKE IT FOR GRANTED

No two elections are the same. In fact, what has worked in the past may not be what works in the future. Can't you feel things changing out there? Your first re-election campaign can be your most vulnerable, so run a fully organized campaign. Demonstrate what you have done, how you helped people, and what you still want to accomplish for your district.

Assemble your kitchen cabinet again and think of people who may be good additions for a re-election race. Have your team review your volunteer and donor lists to ensure their information is up to date, and think of who else you can add (or remove) to your lists now that you've made new alliances.

In your re-election campaign, dare to be a little unpredictable. Ask yourself how you can reach voters but in more interesting ways. Challenge yourself to be inventive by showing your team and voters that you won't fall victim to a stale re-election campaign. If you always send a press release announcing your candidacy, why not do a series of videos around town? If you're a mayor and your town gives the same awards each year to veterans, why not have a reception and invite their families? If you make a social media post for young people who have a school achievement, why not write

In your re-election campaign, dare to be a little unpredictable.

them a letter addressed to the family for a more personal touch? Think about carrying out the same efforts in different, more creative, ways.

BLOCK CAPTAIN STRUCTURE

Campaigns are fleeting, office holders come and go, but organizing is forever, and can get better in time. In fact, I'd like to take you back to the year 1840, when Abraham Lincoln wrote the following to his supporters well before he became president of the United States:

> Our intention is to organize the whole state, so that every Whig can be brought to the polls in the coming Presidential contest. We cannot do this, however,

without your cooperation; and as we do our duty, so we shall expect you to do yours. After due delibera-tion, the following is the plan of organization, and the duties required of each county committee.

- To divide their county into small districts, and to appoint in each a subcommittee, whose duty it shall be to make a perfect list of all the voters in their respective districts, and to ascertain with certainty for whom they will vote. If they meet with men who are doubtful as to the man they will support, such voters should be designated in separate lines, with the name of the man they will probably support.

- It will be the duty of said subcommittee to keep a constant watch on the doubtful voters, and from time to time have them talked to by those in whom they have the most confidence, and also to place in their hands such documents as will enlighten and influence them.

- It will also be their duty to report to you, at least once a month, the progress they are making, and on election days, see that every Whig is brought to the polls.

In this writing, Abraham Lincoln was creating a block captain structure to ensure there was a "perfect" field effort. He understood the importance of having your finger on the pulse of public senti-ment. A block captain strategy is a tried-and-true approach to polit-ical organizing literally person by person, block by block, town by town using relational organizing.

Think of your municipality and break it down by district. These districts are where your polling places are, though you may call them a ward or a precinct. Then, break it down one level further to neighborhoods. Depending on how dense the area is, you can divide each neighborhood into blocks, like this:

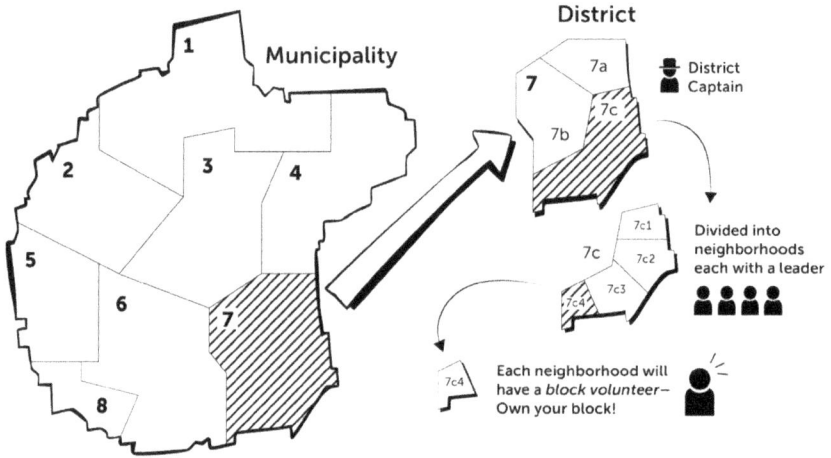

In each of those blocks, have a point person who will lead outreach efforts for this area. Usually, a political party will have a ward or district leader, so you are using this existing structure but breaking it down further. Working together, these organizers will create a web of interactions with residents for meaningful community organizing.

Your campaign, or political party, should create an operation where teams are on the ground talking to voters year-round. Imagine a knock at the door in the spring to hear about what's on their mind in a thoughtful way, and you don't ask for anything! Then, another time you knock on their door and ask about a local issue like education funding, or a new development proposed to solicit their thoughts, and you don't ask for anything more. These types of genuine conversations where you share personal stories will develop into relationships over time.

As you talk to people, you can still target voters as we outlined; but you do not need to be so prescriptive in your approach. Since you are not in the crunch of a campaign, you can more freely talk to those who may never vote for a candidate like you, or those who only vote in those presidential-year races. Of course, you should log their responses, but we are not there to talk *at* them. We are canvassing because we are curious about their thoughts, and we want to listen. Best of all, we are meeting people right where they are and having an ongoing conversation with them.

Sometimes, this kind of organizing has been referred to as deep canvassing, and it originated with LGBTQ+ community leaders who knew we needed to make authentic connections with voters if we were going to turn public opinion on ballot measures like marriage equality. When people talk about how quickly states moved in support of marriage equality, and ultimately for the United States Supreme Court to rule favorably on it, it is in part because of this organizing work that changed minds and changed hearts.

Your campaign, or political party, should create an operation where teams are on the ground talking to voters year-round.

Voters need time to rethink positions, and do not appreciate being told they are blatantly wrong from the get-go. In fact, that's a way to turn them off for good. With year-round organizing, or deep canvassing, it's more about the quality of a conversation than the quantity of how many people you can talk to. This is not about a quick conversation asking for a vote, but playing for the long game, and returning to community members; understanding positions they have held, or perhaps were even passed onto them. In-person respectful conversations are where you ask about opinions, listen, and have an exchange that may move people to think differently, and process beliefs in new ways over time.

We know people are busy, and you may not have volunteers for a full effort, but you'd be wise to start with some level of this block

★ ★ ★

Voters need time to rethink positions, and do not appreciate being told they are blatantly wrong from the get-go.

captain strategy and grow it, even if it's uneven across your district. Start somewhere, and scale it up over time. There are several benefits to this approach:

- Creates unparalleled knowledge of your residents, and keeps their information current
- Grows your lists of volunteers as new people are offering to help
- Builds a self-sustaining structure that you can tailor for each neighborhood
- Increases awareness of who cares about what, so you know who to approach when a certain issue arises
- Shows voters that you and your party truly care about people by creating this sustainable relationship
- Improves candidate recruitment as you are talking to more people; saving time by eliminating the panic to find candidates at the last minute
- Means you are never without a task for volunteers

When election time comes, your supporters are already tapped into the neighborhoods. It takes time, energy, and resources, but you'll be better for it, and so will our democracy. Year-round organizing leads to really commanding the ground in your district, understanding voters' attitudes on issues, and increasing participation through respectful conversations that build rapport.

Your captains who lead these efforts can be party members, family of party members, elected officials and those in their networks, and even people thinking of running for office in the future. With a block captain strategy carrying out this work, you'll be organizing in advanced ways.

One of the efforts I started for our Connecticut Democratic Party was an "Unsung Hero Campaign," where people could nominate others who may not have made the headlines in the campaign but helped write the story. These were the workers; the volunteers who gave so much of themselves in a campaign. It allowed people to be nominated, and then I personally called the unsung hero to simply say thank you; no other agenda or requests, just to share how grateful we were that they were a part of our team. Be sure you are thanking people personally if they are volunteering time and talents for your year-round organizing.

PARTY BUILDING IDEAS

I've worked with local parties that are staying ahead of the curve by bringing in new people, challenging themselves with new ideas, and building an organization to last. Not everything they try may work, but they are constantly improving and testing operations for the strongest possible organization. Leaders of these organizations are not afraid to be uncomfortable and deserve praise for trying new things to ensure they continue to win.

Other local parties will have a different posture: things are good enough, so let's maintain it. This is a safe short-term plan but be mindful that you may be opening yourself up to future atrophy, where there is a gradual decline in effectiveness. When we rest on our laurels and celebrate the wins of yesteryear, we are not pushing for more people, ideas, and support. Over time, a core group will do a little less as they are pleased with the status quo. For districts where the partisan divide is so strong in their favor, they may be in a position to continue to win without much effort. However, this posture is a future vulnerability.

Then, there are parties who are struggling to activate. There could be many reasons for this, including a lack of succession plans when leaders leave, little effort to reach new people, a strong partisan divide against you in your district, or the party not operating in this digital environment. This can be a delicate topic as leadership is under pressure and needs help, but we must realize this is like any other organization; we need people who believe in our values to join and bring their ideas to create an organization that is growing. We are in the people business, so by shutting others out and crouching inward, we are choosing to shrink. *Spoiler alert: That's not a long-term winning strategy.*

While working with party leadership, find new ways to reach people to let your district know the party is alive and well. I have seen local groups be disheartened by recent election losses, and a defeatist attitude begins to sour efforts. I have watched some turn this around by brushing themselves off and trying new approaches, and welcoming young people who want to help, which enhanced party efforts. Here are thirty ways you can reinvigorate local party efforts year-round:

1. Have a listening session among current members and welcome new ideas to grow the party; some may have been thinking of an idea but have yet to share it.
2. Send a postcard to those registered to your party about your monthly meetings and invite them. Once someone new joins, get to know them and welcome them to join again. Be sure to get their information so you are constantly growing your list.

3. Mail or email invites to a free event, like a campaign kick-off, watch party, or social event. Who doesn't love a free invite to a party? Use key moments in the campaign to invite people out.

4. Start an email list and send emails monthly with updates on your group's efforts to demonstrate the work you are doing. At every opportunity, collect people's email addresses so you can keep in touch. If someone contacts you via social media, ask for their information, and add them to your list.

5. Reinvigorate meetings by moving through business first, and then adding a task, like postcard writing or bringing in speakers to create interest. Each meeting could have a different theme, adding curiosity among membership about the next meeting.

6. In meetings, be sure you have time for new ideas and an open floor for people to speak freely. You can call it "talk of the town," so people hear what's happening locally, including your boards and commissions.

7. Find ways to support local office holders, including attending a public hearing, writing a social media post, or letter to the editor about their positive work.

8. Find a volunteer who enjoys social media, and give them access to the social media pages so they may post regularly. Posting on a party's social media page does not need to be intimidating; just look at nearby towns that do it well and replicate that with your message.

9. Host a pizza party, dessert night, or drinks at someone's home when there is work to do, like stuffing envelopes, phone banking, or even a brainstorming session for an event you want to hold. Work together to make the process fun and social again.

10. Volunteer in the community in nonpartisan ways, showing your group that you can transcend politics and simply help

your community. Others will notice this, and you'll reach people who are not already attuned to politics.

11. Challenge existing members to bring just one new person to the next meeting. This is a reasonable challenge and can have a big impact.

12. Do you have people who are intimidated by becoming a formal member of your committee? Create associate member roles where they have no obligation to attend meetings (or vote), but they can test the waters as they get to know the group. You can even assign them a mentor within the group so newcomers feel more welcomed.

13. Identify members who are dedicated to your mission, and delegate tasks to them. Over time, you will build a team, and soon a structure of leaders who are carrying out the work will form.

14. Target new people in town and develop an outreach effort to encourage them to register to vote. You can go door to door on streets where you know a home was recently sold, or use local data to find who is new to town. You may follow up with a piece of mail welcoming them to the community and informing them about your local group.

15. Create or re-evaluate your committee structure so it represents where people are interested. For example, committees for fundraising, issues and press, and recruitment.

16. Approach area high schools and colleges about forming political clubs, and let young people know about your group through student leaders and young political groups.

17. Think about people you have gotten involved (even people who asked for a lawn sign or gave a contribution for the first time) and recruit them to play a more active role.

18. Gather with party and community leaders and make a list of known teachers, first responders, business owners, advocates, and involved community members who may align with

your political party. This is a base of potential candidates in the future.

19. Once you have prospective candidates identified, offer a community meeting open to all to learn about running for office, where current elected officials will talk about their work and answer questions from those who want to get more involved.

20. Let candidates know you expect them to bring at least one new person to the group and make a contribution. If candidates are invested, you'll be growing the party, and the candidate will now have a friend there, too.

21. Create or identify an existing event you can enhance, and make that your signature event you can build on year to year.

22. Implement a block captain strategy as outlined, starting in the areas of the district where you have the most supporters ready to organize.

23. Host an annual holiday party or winter volunteer opportunity, helping those in need and offering your group something to do *after* the election.

24. Run letters to the editor asking people to attend a local political meeting, informing them that your group welcomes new people, and encouraging community members to attend local board meetings.

25. Make it a goal to run someone in every race, even if a person is just putting their name on the ballot; give voters choices!

26. Be sure to have consistent branding on your website, printed materials, and social media so that your group looks professional and welcoming. Ensure your website has updated information, and meetings are posted.

27. If you have members who have been involved for a long time, and it's preventing new members from joining because you're at capacity of the allowed amount of members, create emerita roles for your lifetime members. Rather than

turning people away, find ways to pull up more chairs to the table and bring people in.

28. Contact complimentary groups and your state political party and see what efforts they have planned for areas of collaboration, like peaceful protests or organizing days.

29. Work with experienced campaigners in your area and hold trainings for candidates. You can even collaborate with nearby towns to share organizing best practices.

30. Look for ways to be intentional about bringing people to the table who are not already part of the group. This could be diverse perspectives like people from a certain neighborhood, young people, various racial backgrounds, veterans, small business owners, and more. During a meeting, look around and then think to yourself, *Who from our community is not reflected in this room?* Then, get to work.

★★★

During a meeting, look around and then think to yourself, *Who from our community is not reflected in this room?*

There are a lot of ideas here, and you may feel like you need a whole team to make each happen. Try starting with just one of these ideas, and you may be surprised by the result. Remember, one person can make a difference, especially that first person who begins the effort.

Collectively, through blending the experience of veteran campaigners with fresh ideas, welcoming people, good communications, interesting meetings, fun events, and being present in the community, you can turn a tired party into one that is buzzing with potential to win. It won't happen overnight, but with time and attention, month by month, two new people will double to four, new candidates will step forward, and you'll be growing your party.

For more on year-round organizing, visit **OrganizingtoWin.com**

GIVE THEM
Hope

★ ★ ★

R unning for public office is a lesson in listening and understanding those kitchen table conversations: voters' fears, frustrations, needs and wants, and hopes for their future. Succeeding in
public office means you can weave all that together and make government actually work for people, and improve working people's
livelihoods—increasing freedoms and economic opportunity—by
making life better.

America continues to see a widening gap of economic dispar-
ity, with rapid advancements in technology, leading to corporations
accelerating the use of automation and artificial intelligence to replace
what were once human jobs. If you don't believe me, visit a manufacturing floor and watch a 3D printer do the job that a team of workers
would pour their sweat into. Combine that with corporate greed, rising costs, and stagnant wages while people are working harder than
ever to make ends meet, and it leads to real economic anxiety.

Sit around the kitchen table in a working-class community
like mine in the Naugatuck Valley, and you'll find people who feel
left behind. They believe this government focuses on the needs
of billionaires, while so much of their paycheck goes to the cost

of living: healthcare, housing, energy, and childcare. Hearing positive indicators about the economy only makes people who are living paycheck to paycheck feel worse; dissatisfied about those in power. This leads to anger toward public officials, often turning voters off so they no longer vote, thinking it won't make *any* difference.

A 2025 Wall Street Journal/NORC Research Center study found 69 percent of Americans said they thought the American dream no longer holds true, or that it never was true. Only 25 percent thought they had a good chance of improving their current standard of living, with an overwhelming sense of pessimism around the American economy and one's ability to get ahead.

As people are busy working or caring for young children, elderly parents, and the responsibilities of life, they are inundated with misinformation and disinformation, not knowing what to believe as they see political bickering on social media. Some think that *every* politician is the same, which could not be further from the truth. Some may think, *Why even bother voting?* not realizing many races come down to just a difference of a few votes. Some wince at the thought of politics, and proclaim *I don't do politics*, which does not stop politics from happening *to them* as they render themselves powerless. Given the economic pressures people face, some may start to think, *What do I have to lose?* And so, they will vote for someone who promises to be a disruptor, even if that candidate has no intention of helping them.

That belief has permeated our politics, with some candidates using anger as currency to hold power by eliminating freedoms, stymying institutions, and poisoning public discourse as they hand government to a favored few. Like burning embers on the ground, they would rather strike a match and throw it, fanning the flames to ensure they capitalize on people's frustrations. Some work to break the very departments they lead, and then decry just how broken the government is. I don't believe this represents the best of our democracy, do you?

Keep in mind people are spending less time in group activities, whether that's in school groups, sports, or community activities. People are on their phones scrolling and not physically with friends as much as they use to be, meaning less in-person socialization. Post the COVID-19 pandemic, there are increased work-from-home options, and everyone is more isolated these days.

There is a loneliness to feeling overlooked, and opponents—with the help of a fractured media environment—are surrounding voters with messages as if they are sitting on their couch, keeping them occupied by pointing fingers at *others* to blame as they stay lonely and angry. So long as they continue to disengage these voters, they will keep pumping them with misinformation to distort and control. Opponents realize if they can poison the public discourse and make it *so miserable*, they'll turn people off to vote, thereby weakening public participation and threatening our democracy for good. We must reverse this.

Let's be clear: A cynic would laugh if they heard you and I were talking about how to campaign, as if you want to become the politician they see on TV! That's because there's *so much* skepticism about this government and those who are a part of it. Pew Research Center reports only 22 percent of Americans say they trust the government to do the right thing. Their findings point to an erosion of trust in institutions, science, and especially those in office. With regard to political parties, it's just as bad. The major political parties are underwater in their popularity; with people viewing both major parties more unfavorably than favorably.

Our democracy is worth fighting for, and it starts with you. **When others are enraged, you stay engaged.**

The answer for those who have lost trust in government should not be to erase it, but rather make it better; make it work for people once again. I've seen what can be possible in politics, and you will too. Let's break through this cynicism together by running for office and being the change so many wish to see in their government. *Our democracy is worth fighting for, and it starts with you.* When others are enraged, you stay engaged. We are in a country of self-governance and you have the opportunity to make government work for the people.

So, what are you going to do? Bring your campaign back to the kitchen table and root it in an economic message for working people. Candidates, office holders, and staff have an opportunity to make things better for people:

1. Recognize people feel left behind and want authentic representation.
2. Know you can make a difference, especially at the local and state levels.
3. Survey the community and political environment by listening and learning.
4. Get involved by showing up in your community and volunteering.
5. Participate in your local party and decide to run for office.
6. Get out the vote through a rigorous targeted field effort.
7. Raise the funds to compete in this campaign.
8. Communicate—in many ways—to voters with your message.
9. When in office, build coalitions to get things done for people.
10. Create something special and bring others along with year-round organizing.

ELECTIONS MATTER

The reality is there is no such thing as an "off" election year. Elections are happening every year, and politics is not something that can simply be turned off or turned on. It's always happening and can be strengthened or weakened based on those who are participating, especially those who take on the responsibility of running and serving in office.

Look, the dynamics we are dealing with can be dizzying. Young people have been told everything that happened in their life so far has been a *once-in-a-lifetime crisis*: from global conflicts, to financial fallout and the Great Recession, an epidemic of overdoses and gun violence, a devastating pandemic, change in climate with increasing natural disasters, to an affordability crisis. Yet still, young people show up to get involved, ready to engage in politics.

When some win elections by pointing fingers at others, you can earn support by pointing toward the future; showing a path forward of how you would improve lives.

As you talk with voters, listen respectfully to their concerns, and connect them to your personal story and *your Why*. When some win elections by pointing fingers at others, you can earn support by pointing toward the future; showing a path forward of how you would improve lives. People may be skeptical about government and politics, but you will show them you are an authentic candidate making a positive difference in your district. You ran because you wanted to fix, achieve, create, or strengthen something for your community.

Your candidacy can help renew the belief that authentic people are running for office and responding to people's needs. From the hands of a factory worker to a crop farmer, small businesswoman and the next generation of voters, you'll be a candidate who can sit down at the kitchen table, talk about what matters, and then make good on the promise that you will deliver for the people of your district. In fact, *your Why* may become the reason why someone decides to vote for the first time. Your efforts can lead to improving the local turnout—3 out of 10 eligible voters casting a ballot—using the strategies we discussed. Then, you'll continue those conversations after the election for year-round organizing. When you do this, you won't just be campaigning for office, you'll be strengthening our democracy with each election. Doesn't that give you hope?

You will play a role in restoring the public's trust that the government can actually work for people—those who voted for you, those who did not, and even the cynics.

Are you ready to meet the moment?

CITIZEN
Government

★ ★ ★

J uly 4, 2026, marks the 250th anniversary of the United States of America. One of the signers of the Declaration of Independence was one of the most influential citizens in our history, Benjamin Franklin. When he was asked what type of government the Constitutional Convention adopted, he said, "A republic, *if you can keep it.*" A republic is a state where power is held by people who elect their representatives. This meant a government without a king that was by and for the people. The Declaration of Independence was a self-governing statement of our new American ideals—mainly life, liberty, and the pursuit of happiness.

The American story is one of mistakes and advancements, setbacks and breakthroughs, missed opportunities and milestones. We've led the world with innovations across academia, science, and business. We've made breakthroughs in technology, built the transcontinental railroad and highway system, expanded the right to vote, enacted historic social safety net programs, protected workers and enacted the five-day work week, and ensured safety for food, water, and air quality. From the Civil Rights Movement to the Suffragettes; the Labor Movement and the fight for marriage equality; to celebrating our history as a country of immigrants, and supporting women's bodily choices, people have organized time and time again. At the core of each of these movements is the American citizen.

Our democracy needs care; it thrives when citizens participate, and it weakens when citizens don't. When our democracy is ignored, or faced with threats, you must wonder if it can withstand such treatment since our institutions are only as strong as those individuals within them. If we are to strengthen democracy, we must participate, run for office, and step into leadership roles.

If we are to strengthen democracy, we must participate, run for office, and step into leadership roles.

The mindset of leadership has changed with new generations taking power. Leadership used to be viewed as a top-down hierarchy with strict controls. Because, in part, people feel left behind by those at the top, they are turning to the change-makers in the center of the action. Now, leadership is seen as being accessible, and focused on getting something done for people. Leaders are those at the center of collaboration, serving as activists from the core rather than bygone managers at the top. This has the potential to reinvigorate our city halls, state capitols, and instituions as we forge an economic future that functions for working people. People, particularly young people, are demanding action, and their participation will renew our democracy through an engaged citizenry.

Every year, we hear the words: *This is the most important election of our lifetime.* It sounds like hyperbole, but it's true because with each passing election, we have one more chance to elect the right people to critical roles. Would we really say: *Actually, this election is not important.* With low voter turnout and given most Americans feel the country is heading in the wrong direction—our democracy *is* at stake. The spirit of America is with its people, and it is one that believes we are striving toward a *more* perfect union. So, what are the benchmarks for reaching a more perfect union? It's elections, and the next election *is* the most important in our life.

With this in mind, I decided to run for the national committee of my own party, the Democratic National Committee, the oldest continuing political party in the United States of America. Running for the DNC was not because I possess a blind loyalty to the party, but rather I understand that to make change you must put yourself and your ideas forward. The race was competitive, but through person-to-person organizing, I was elected in the summer of 2025 to an at-large seat and am working to bring reforms and more organizing ideas to the DNC. Running for a position among a membership organization carries many of the lessons we discussed but is focused on a relatively small number of individuals compared to a district's electorate. When I addressed the members before the vote, I said, ". . . The DNC should be accessible, collaborative, develop candidate pipelines, and offer a bold economic vision for working people. If something is broken, let's be the ones to fix it. I ask for your vote as an outsider who learned how to organize to win. Our country is in crisis, our party is at a critical moment, and we must make life better."

Every week a young person will message me asking, "Have a few minutes to chat?" Undoubtedly, they tell me they want to get involved by running for office to fight for liberties they feel are under attack. I remind them of the lessons I've learned so far, and here's one more: I found when you strengthen your community by participating, you'll find you strengthened your own purpose in life. In other words, helping others will help you. That's because in giving a voice to others, you'll find a voice you never knew you had as you speak up for those who need it most. Public service can fulfill you, bring happiness, and actually change *your* life.

There is no shortage of issues to work on: People want the largest corporations to pay their share in taxes, and demand an economic agenda rooted in affordability that addresses the increasing cost of living so families have a fair shot. People who work one job should have the wherewithal to have an affordable home in a safe neighborhood, with quality healthcare, and economic security for their family. There may be local issues that were a part of *your Why*, from creating housing to developing your downtown in a thoughtful way, investing in infrastructure to addressing childcare needs. There are many areas where we need smart people like you to play in the space where policy meets politics. *And that space is called organizing.* Starting locally, you can listen to people, keep your head down doing good work, and form a campaign. With so much at stake, you must be your authentic self and fight for the needs of people through public policy.

THE JOURNEY OF PUBLIC SERVICE

Not long ago, I was asked to be a part of a new show on our state's CBS affiliate, WFSB, along with former Connecticut House of Representatives Republican Leader Themis Klarides, an experienced policymaker who knows the state legislature very well. I was billed as the Democratic Party strategist as we discussed live on air the local, state, and federal issues impacting families every week. In the first episode, seated under the bright lights of a TV studio, the cameras blinked a red light, and veteran host Kara Sundlun said, "Welcome to the first episode of Capitol Rundown! I am here with my *insiders*, Themis Klarides and Jimmy Tickey."

I never studied political science, was not from a political family, and had no experience when I got involved in my hometown. I often was the youngest, the newest, or the first (but not the last). Through organizing, I saw what could be possible as I managed campaigns, served in government, and advanced in the political arena. I had become knowledgeable about political matters, could explain them concisely, and was now reporting my take on television.

It's not that the outsider transforms into some insider. When you are effective in this space, others will position themselves around you; and suddenly the outsider is no longer watching from afar but is surrounded. *When did this happen?* Through organizing,

If you are authentic in your approach, then winning the day does not mean you won it for yourself, but you won the day for the people you represent.

you'll be standing in the center of action as others look to you for guidance, especially in uncertain times. Before you know it, you will be teaching others who feel like they don't belong that with authenticity, some grit, and a plan, they will be ready.

Working together, we can reform broken systems, deliver for our communities, and get results for people. When you advocate for people not knowing if it will be successful, you are fighting for those in your community who you may never even meet. That's the point of electing great people, so they can do good for their community. On this journey you will have attacks, surprises, and setbacks—and in those moments you must keep going. If you are authentic in your approach, then winning the day does not mean you won it for yourself, but you won the day for the people you represent.

To those who feel on the outside, those who speak out against the status quo, and those whose voice is not reflected in government yet—look inside yourself and know you are needed. Then, look around and get to work. If you still believe that our democracy is worth fighting for, then it starts with you, right now. Engage in the political arena, whether that's getting involved in your town, advocating for legislation, volunteering on a campaign, working in politics, or charting your own unique path. Then, meet people where they are, and run for office. When you run, don't dust off a playbook from generations ago but use the strategies we've discussed. It won't

★★★

When we fight for the many and do the hard work of year-round organizing, we build something everlasting.

be easy, and that's because there's not a perfect way to organize: It's part art and part science, and you can make it your own. Kitchen table by kitchen table, with mobilization, money, and a message, we are managing the chaos, getting out the vote, and organizing to win.

Working people need a win, and you can give them that hope— then deliver on it. When we fight for the many and do the hard work of year-round organizing, we build something everlasting. As you achieve this, you will realize you never were an imposter, but rather were right where you needed to be all along. A journey of public service unlocks something inside yourself as helping others gives you a unique purpose in life. In the future, others will build upon that legacy of service when you welcome them into the political arena. Now that's *special*, and something no one can take from you.

Since we began this conversation with a secret, let's end with one: The best way to learn the lessons of politics and government is by *actually* playing a role in politics and government. It's up to all of us, and our future is in your hands as we look to the next election.

This may be our conclusion, but I know your journey is just starting. In this political arena, some doors will be wide open for you, and other doors are slightly cracked so you can work your way in. There will be times doors are shut to you, and that's when you start knocking. The time has come to get off the sidelines and participate in the oldest American effort for the last 250 years: a citizen government.

LESSONS: A NOTE
From the Author

★ ★ ★

While at home on a rainy Saturday morning in March 2024, an idea came to me as I was reviewing training materials I created for candidates. I thought there must be a way I could document the lessons I had been voluntarily teaching to candidates, and thought of developing a handbook that could help people run for office.

I began typing what I knew from my nonprofit, local, state, and federal campaign experiences; as well as lessons learned from thousands of conversations I've had. I reviewed notes, documents, and began to write in chronological order, thinking about how one gets involved, forming the campaign, running for office, and all the moving pieces toward Election Day and beyond. Bullet points became sentences and paragraphs grew into chapters, as organizing lessons flooded my mind. I don't pretend to know *all* the answers (I was self-taught and never studied political science), but this represented my experiences and recollections, and no artificial intelligence or ghost writers were involved. Months later, I had captured what I wanted to say, and it was sixty thousand words. I thought, *Well, if I ever need content to help a candidate, I can pull from these lessons.* The document sat on my computer, and there it would stay.

With the election year of 2024 and through 2025, there were many political events which rocked our democracy. My phone began to buzz. Young people were messaging me asking for advice, and seasoned politicos were contacting me to brainstorm. People wanted to organize, and they needed direction; they wanted to win, but they needed leadership.

Similar to a campaign, I surveyed the environment and found there are *many* political theory and memoir books, but *very few* how-to campaign books from those who have lived it. For young people, *barely any at all.* I reread my manuscript as Americans peacefully protested in mass. Americans saw the power of organizing, and I thought, *Imagine what our democracy could look like with a more engaged citizenry.* I realized now *is* the time if there ever was one to remind people what I wrote about: We need a citizen government that is focused on making life better for the many. Further, I wanted to teach how good year-round organizing can build for a stronger democracy one authentic candidate at a time. I could have made this book more partisan, but when dealing with running for local office, the potholes don't care about party, they just need to be fixed. To enhance learning, relevant anecdotes, call-out quotes, whiteboard infographics, and companion resources were developed.

In August 2025, a column across Connecticut's Hearst papers read: "Tickey lives politics from every angle." I never thought I would be involved in politics; I just liked the feeling of voting with my parents as a kid. I've learned the feeling of helping others is even better, so after holding this close to me for nearly two years, I moved forward with a how-to book written as a conversation, just you and me. If you listened closely, you heard a hopeful story.

As a kid, I did not dare dream of getting elected to office, serving in party leadership, marrying a man I love, or writing a book to help others. This project encapsulates a period of hard work and happiness during challenging political times.

THANK YOU

Thank you to my mom and dad for supporting me no matter what idea I come up with next. Thank you to my sister Nicole and her family—Ben, Magnolia, Delilah, and Ruby—for their love and encouragement.

Thank you to my husband Sam, who insisted I include personal stories to complement the teachings, which made for a better book.

To Mary Ann and Chris Far, Bob Lally, Dave Gioiello, and Elaine Matto—thank you for welcoming me to local politics. To the people and families of Shelton, and to those who play a role in our beloved All-American Naugatuck Valley—from the volunteers to civic and nonprofit leaders—thank you for trusting in me at such a young age.

I am grateful to Susan Bysiewicz, Rosa DeLauro, and Jim Himes for your confidence in me, and for setting an example of dedicated public service. Thank you to Connecticut's incredible federal delegation, hardworking Democrats across the State of Connecticut, and Democratic National Committee members whom I have worked alongside.

Thank you to my Channel 3 WFSB Capitol Rundown counterparts, Kara Sundlun and Themis Klarides for meaningful discussion during divisive times—and to those who watch our balanced conversations.

To all those I've learned from, as well as Nancy DiNardo, Jennifer Lamb, Chris Lyddy, and Erick Russell – I am thankful for your friendship. Very special thanks to Kevin Alvarez, Stephen Blinder, Will Haskell, Tyler Mack, Michelle Moreno-Silva, Danny Salemme, and Jessica Stram for reviewing segments of this book so thoughtfully. Thank you to Jenn Grace for guiding me in this publishing effort, and to all those who assisted with this project.

I will never know whose hands are holding this book in 2026 and beyond, so I hope you use these lessons to get involved, run for office, and occupy space in the political arena with your authentic self. Together, we are organizing to win.

ABOUT
the Author

★ ★ ★

J immy Tickey is a trusted political voice in Connecticut, providing guidance to local, state, and federal campaigns and political parties. An At-Large Member of the Democratic National Committee, Tickey has been elected as the Connecticut Democratic Party Vice Chair since 2022, leading training efforts, and appears on Connecticut television as a Democratic strategist.

A native of Connecticut's Naugatuck Valley, Tickey has served in local office since 2011 in the City of Shelton, where his electoral support broke records. His involvement has included the board of directors for the Boys & Girls Club of the Lower Naugatuck Valley, Valley United Way, Griffin Hospital, Connecticut's League of Conservation Voters, Planned Parenthood of Southern New England, and co-creator of Celebrate Shelton.

Tickey's professional tenure includes District Director for Congressman Jim Himes, Campaign Manager for Congresswoman Rosa DeLauro, and Senior Advisor to Lieutenant Governor Susan Bysiewicz. He has helped countless candidates seek local, state, and federal office.

A graduate of Fordham University's Gabelli School of Business in New York, Tickey completed Harvard Kennedy School's Senior Executives in State & Local Government in Massachusetts.

Tickey is married to Samuel Carmody and resides in Connecticut where he can always be found working on a project around the house and garden with their rescue dog, Riley Sunshine.

Tickey released his first book, *Organizing to Win: The Art & Science of Running for Office*, at the age of thirty-eight.

RESOURCES

★ ★ ★

Learn about these organizing topics and more with downloadable how-to guides at *OrganizingToWin.com*:

- Deciding to Run & Win
- Reaching Voters
- Door Knocking 101
- Fundraising Strategies
- Developing a Budget
- Effective Scheduling
- Year-Round Organizing

REFERENCES

"Black Women in American Politics 2025." 2025. Rutgers. https://cawp. rutgers.edu/sites/default/files/2025-07/Black%20Women%20 in%20Politics%202025_Final.pdf.

"BrainyQuote." 2025. BrainyQuote. 2025. https://www.brainyquote. com/quotes/mario_cuomo_111605.

"Case Closed in Shelton Corruption Probe." Valley Independent Sentinel. May 28, 2014. https://valley.newhavenindependent.org/article/ case_closed_in_shelton_corruption_probe.

Center for American Women and Politics. "Current Numbers." Cawp. rutgers.edu. Eagleton Institute of Politics. 2025. https://cawp. rutgers.edu/facts/current-numbers.

"CNN Poll Political Parties." n.d. https://s3.documentcloud.org/ documents/25563079/cnn-poll-political-parties.pdf.

Deane, Claudia. "Americans' Deepening Mistrust of Institutions." Pewtrusts.org. The Pew Charitable Trusts. October 17, 2024. https://www.pewtrusts.org/en/trend/archive/fall-2024/americans-deepening-mistrust-of-institutions.

Denizet-Lewis, Benoit. "How Do You Change Voters' Minds? Have a Conversation." *The New York Times*, April 7, 2016, sec. Magazine. https://www.nytimes.com/2016/04/10/magazine/how-do-you-change-voters-minds-have-a-conversation.html.

Einav, Michal, and Malka Margalit. 2023. "Loneliness before and after COVID-19: Sense of Coherence and Hope as Coping Mechanisms." *International Journal of Environmental Research and Public Health* 20 (10): 5840–40. https://doi.org/10.3390/ijerph20105840.

Green, Donald P, and Alan S Gerber. *Get out the Vote: How to Increase Voter Turnout*. Washington, D.C.: Brookings Institution Press, 2019.

Haar, Dan. "A Rising Democrat Wins an Extra National Committee Seat for CT." *CT Insider*, August 26, 2025, www.ctinsider.com/politics/ article/jimmy-tickey-ct-democratic-party-21016591.php. Accessed October 6, 2025.

Jones, Jeffrey M. 2025. "LGBTQ+ Identification in U.S. Rises to 9.3%." Gallup. February 20, 2025. https://news.gallup.com/poll/656708/ lgbtq-identification-rises.aspx.

"Local Journalism Collapse Deeper Than Previously Known, Study Suggests." PRSA.org. July 17, 2025. https://prsay.prsa.org/2025/ 07/17/local-journalism-collapse-deeper-than-previously-known- study-suggests/.

Martinez, Gracie, and Jeffrey S. Passel. 2025. "Facts about the U.S. Black Population." Pew Research Center. January 23, 2025. https://www. pewresearch.org/race-and-ethnicity/fact-sheet/facts-about-the-us- black-population/.

Martínez, José Luis. "CT 2023 Election: Voter Turnout Percentages from across the State." CT Mirror. November 10, 2023. https://ctmirror. org/2023/11/10/ct-2023-election-voter-turnout/.

Mayko, Michael P. "Federal Corruption Probe in Shelton Moving Forward." Connecticut Post. October 21, 2010. https://www.ctpost. com/local/article/federal-corruption-probe-in-shelton-moving- forward-715779.php.

"NBC News Decision Desk Poll Results." Google.com. June 16, 2025. https://docs.google.com/viewerng/viewer?url=https://WFMJ. images.worldnow.com/library/5d0d7334-83d2-439f-85fb- 335b44cbe709.pdf.

"Papers of Abraham Lincoln." Papersofabrahamlincoln.org. 2018. https://papersofabrahamlincoln.org/documents/D200214.

Reyes, Yacob. "Latinos Are a Flourishing Force on Ballots." Axios. February 3, 2022. https://www.axios.com/2022/02/03/latinos-in-office-election-democrats.

"September 17, 1787: A Republic, If You Can Keep It (U.S. National Park Service)." n.d. Nps.gov. Accessed September 21, 2023. https://www.nps.gov/articles/000/constitutionalconvention-september17.htm.

"Shelton Building Official Admits Lying to Grand Jury during Public Corruption Probe." FBI. 2025. https://archives.fbi.gov/archives/newhaven/press-releases/2010/nh010610.htm.

"The State of Civics Education in the General Populace." Americanbar.org. 2024. https://www.americanbar.org/groups/public_interest/election_law/american-democracy/our-work/state-civics-education-general-populace/.

Timotija, Filip. "Pessimism about Economy at Record Highs in New Survey." *The Hill*, September 2, 2025, thehill.com/business/5481068-pessimism-economy-record-high-survey/amp/. Accessed October 6, 2025.

"Tully Message Box: Use It for Your Political Campaign." Thecampaignworkshop.com. 2020. https://www.thecampaignworkshop.com/blog/pillar/political-campaign/tully-message-box.

Winograd, Morley, Michael Hais, and Doug Ross "How Younger Voters Will Impact Elections: Younger Voters Are Poised to Upend American Politics." Brookings. February 27, 2023. https://www.brookings.edu/articles/younger-voters-are-poised-to-upend-american-politics/.